DATE DUE

NO2 9'99			

DEMCO 38-296

Kuwait

CSIS Middle East Dynamic Net Assessment

Kuwait

Recovery and Security
After the Gulf War

Anthony H. Cordesman

WestviewPress

A Division of HarperCollins*Publishers*

Published in 1997 in the United States of America by Westview Press, 5500 Central
Avenue, Boulder, Colorado 80301-2877, and in the United Kingdom by Westview Press, 12
Hid's Copse Road, Cumnor Hill, Oxford OX2 9JJ

Library of Congress Cataloging-in-Publication Data
Cordesman, Anthony H.
   Kuwait : recovery and security after the Gulf War / Anthony H.
Cordesman.
      p.   cm.
   Includes bibliographical references.
   ISBN 0-8133-3243-5 (hc). — ISBN 0-8133-3244-3 (pbk.)
   1. Kuwait—Politics and government.   2. Kuwait—Defenses.
I. Title.
DS247.K88C67   1997
953.6705'3—dc21   96-44401
                                                                                                         CIP

This book was typeset by Letra Libre, 1705 Fourteenth Street, Suite 391, Boulder, Colorado
80302.

The paper used in this publication meets the requirements of the American National Standard for Permanence of Paper for Printed Library Materials Z39.48-1984.

10   9   8   7   6   5   4   3   2   1

Contents

Tables and Illustrations

Maps

Preface

This volume is part of an ongoing dynamic net assessment of the Gulf. The project was conceived by David Abshire and Richard Fairbanks of the Center for Strategic and International Studies, and focuses on the foreign policy, military forces, politics, economics, energy sector, and internal security of each Gulf state, and US strategy and power projection capabilities in the Gulf. Separate volumes are available on Kuwait, Iran, Iraq, Saudi Arabia, and US forces. Bahrain, Oman, Qatar, and the UAE are combined into a single volume.

Each of these volumes is interlinked to provide comparable data on the current situation and trends in each country, and to portray the overall trends in key areas like the economy and the military balance. The volume on Iran provides a detailed graphic overview of the military trends in the region, but each volume shows how the key economic and military developments in each country relate to the developments in other Gulf countries.

At the same time, this series deliberately emphasizes nation-by-nation analysis. Iran and Iraq clearly deserve separate treatment. The Southern Gulf states are largely independent actors and are driven by separate strategic, political, economic, and military interests. In spite of the creation of the Arab Gulf Cooperation Council (GCC), there is little practical progress in strategic, economic, or military cooperation, and there are serious rivalries and differences of strategic interest between Bahrain, Kuwait, Oman, Qatar, Saudi Arabia, and the UAE. The Southern Gulf cannot be understood in terms of the rhetoric of the Arab Gulf Cooperation Council, or by assuming that developments in Bahrain, Kuwait, Oman, Qatar, Saudi Arabia, and the UAE are similar and these states have an identity of interest.

These Gulf studies are also part of a broader dynamic net assessment of the Middle East, and a separate study is available of the trends in the Arab-Israeli military balance and the peace process. See Anthony H. Cordesman, *Perilous Prospects*, Boulder, Westview, 1996.

Anthony H. Cordesman

Acknowledgments

This volume is part of a six-volume series reporting on a dynamic net assessment of the Gulf. The project was conceived by David Abshire and Richard Fairbanks of the Center for Strategic and International Studies, and is part of a broader dynamic net assessment of the entire Middle East.

The author would like to thank Kimberly Goddes and Kiyalan Batman-glidj for their research and editing help in writing this series, and Thomas Seidenstein and David Hayward for helping to edit each volume.

Many US and international analysts and agencies played a role in commenting on drafts of the manuscript. So did experts in each Southern Gulf country. The author cannot acknowledge these contributions by name or agency but he is deeply grateful. The author would also like to thank his colleagues at the CSIS who reviewed various manuscripts and commented on the analysis. These colleagues include Richard Fairbanks and Arnaud de Borchgrave, and his Co-Director of the Middle East Program, Judith Kipper.

A.H.C.

1

Introduction

Kuwait plays a critical role in any projection of the world's future oil supplies. As of 1994, Kuwait had estimated proven oil reserves of 94.8 to 96.5 billion barrels, or about 8.6% to 9.7% of all world reserves. Most estimates indicated that Kuwait has probable reserves of at least 4 billion barrels more.[1] Many of Kuwait's reserves are easy to extract and have recovery costs of only about $2 a barrel.[2]

Kuwait is also one of the two major oil exporting powers that can rapidly increase production in an emergency, an important fact that will grow steadily over time. The US Department of Energy estimates that Kuwait will expand its production from a little over 2.3 million barrels per day in 1995 to 3.1 (3.0–3.3) million barrels per day in 2000, 3.8 (3.6–4.5) million barrels per day in 2005, and 4.6 (4.0–5.1) million barrels per day in 2010.[3]

At the same time, Kuwait's geography, small size, and limited population make it one of the most vulnerable Gulf states. Its location on Iraq's border has been the source of continuing Iraqi threats, military confrontation, and actual invasion. Its location within a few minutes flying time of Iran has made it equally vulnerable to Iranian threats and pressure. Iranian aircraft attacked Kuwait several times during the Iran-Iraq War. Iranian naval forces attacked tankers and other ships moving to Kuwait. Iranian anti-ship missiles attacked targets in Kuwait's harbors, and Iranian intelligence sponsored bombings and terrorist attacks.

This combination of oil wealth and geographical vulnerability make Kuwait a critical strategic pivot in a net assessment of the Gulf. The ability of Kuwait, its neighbors, and the West to deal with Iraqi intimidation or invasion largely determines the security of the upper Gulf and the containment of Iraq's political and military ambitions.

Strategic Background

Kuwait is located in the far northwestern corner of the upper Gulf between Iraq and Saudi Arabia, and within a short distance of Iran. It is

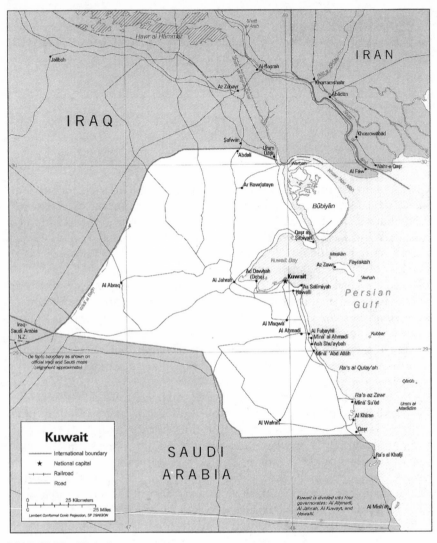

MAP ONE   Kuwait

one of the world's major oil powers, but it has a total area of only 17,800 square kilometers—roughly the size of New Jersey. At its largest point, Kuwait is about 200 kilometers from north to south and 170 kilometers from east to west. It shares a 242 kilometer border with Iraq and a 222 kilometer border with Saudi Arabia. It has a 499 kilometer coastline on the Gulf, and its territory includes nine islands. Bubiyan and Warbah—

two large islands in the north—are uninhabited but are of strategic importance, because they border the Umm Qasr channel, which is Iraq's only waterway with direct access to the Gulf.[4]

Like a number of states in the upper Gulf, Kuwait can trace its history as far back as that of Dilmun. Kuwait's modern history began in the early 1700s, when families from the Bani Utub clan of the Anaizah tribe migrated from Qatar to found the city of Kuwait. In 1765, these tribes chose Sabah al Sabah as their ruling sheik. He was succeeded by his son Abdullah, who was succeeded in turn by his son Jabair.

This line of succession established the tradition that the ruler of Kuwait is to be chosen by a council of the Al Sabah family, after consultation with other leading families. This decision had a major impact on the future of both Qatar and Bahrain. The Al Khalifa family, closely related to the Al Sabahs and a rival for leadership of Kuwait, decided to seek a new power base elsewhere in the Gulf. The Al Khalifas first took control of Qatar and then conquered Bahrain with the aid of the Al Sabahs of Kuwait.

By 1770, Kuwait was a fishing and trading town surrounded by tribal families who engaged in nomadic agriculture. The role of the Al Sabah Sheik consisted largely of negotiating with the Ottoman Empire, surrounding tribes, and other Gulf states. In 1775 the British East India Company made its first contacts with Kuwait. Between 1775 and 1779, the British-operated Persian Gulf-Aleppo Mail Service was diverted through Kuwait from Persian-occupied Basra (today Iraq). At the same time, the rise of the Wahhabis and Al Saud family created a new center of power in Arabia. These developments forced Kuwait to deal increasingly with the British and Al Sauds, as well as the Ottoman Empire. Kuwait had little trade or contact with the Persian Empire at this time.

By the late 1770s, the growing regional competition between Britain, the Ottoman Empire, and the Persian Empire forced Kuwait to choose one of the powers as a patron. In 1871, Abdullah Al Sabah II allied Kuwait with Turkey and took the title of Qaimaqam, or provincial governor, from the Ottoman Sultan. These ties had little practical meaning, however, since the Ottoman Empire did not exert any significant control over Kuwait.

Kuwait ended its ties to the Ottoman Empire in 1896. Abdullah Al Sabah II died in 1892. He was succeeded by Muhammad Al Sabah who died four years later. Al Sabah's death triggered a struggle for power that was eventually won by Mubarak Al Sabah, who killed his brothers during the struggle. Mubarak opposed Turkish influence so when the Ottomans backed his rivals, he approached Britain, which was concerned with the growth of German influence in Turkey, construction of the Berlin-to-Baghdad railway, and plans to link the railway to the port of Kuwait.

As a result, Britain and Kuwait signed a treaty in 1899 that promised Kuwait the British support in return for British control over Kuwait's foreign policy. Sheik Mubarak pledged that neither he nor his successors would cede any territory, or receive the agents or representatives of any foreign power, without the British Government's consent. Britain agreed to grant an annual subsidy to support the Sheik and his heirs and to provide for Kuwait's protection. A British political agent was appointed in 1904, who handled Kuwait's foreign affairs and security. In return, Kuwait enjoyed special treaty relations with Britain.

Although Iraq has made claims to Kuwait as an "inheritor state" to the Ottoman Empire, Turkey had only limited sovereignty over Kuwait for a period of 15 years, while Kuwait's ties to Britain lasted from 1899 until 1961 when Kuwait received full independence. Further, Britain negotiated a treaty with the Ottoman Empire in 1913 that would have regularized its new relationship with Kuwait. The outbreak of World War I prevented this treaty's ratification, but Kuwait's sovereignty received de facto recognition long before Iraq came into existence.

Kuwait's alliance with Britain helped Sheik Mubarak consolidate his power and make his sons its rulers. Sheik Mubarak was succeeded by his son Jabir (1915–17) and subsequently by another son, Salim (1917–21). Subsequent Emirs were descendants of these two brothers. Sheik Ahmed al-Jabir Al Sabah ruled from 1921 until his death in the 1950s. As a result of this long reign, Mubarak's branch of the family became the dominant branch of the Al Sabah family until 1950. This peaceful succession created a new degree of internal stability within Kuwait.

Kuwait did, however, face increasing challenges from the outside. The first challenge came from Saudi Arabia, which attacked north towards Kuwait in 1921, won a major battle at Al Jahrah, less than 40 kilometers from Kuwait City, and threatened to conquer the country. This led to British intervention in 1922, when Sir Percy Cox, the British agent called together the representatives of Kuwait, Britain's newly formed League of Nations mandate, Iraq, and Saudi Arabia (then the Sultanate of Najd). The resulting negotiations led to the Treaty of Muhammara (May 1, 1992) and the Protocol of Uqayr (December 2, 1922).

These two agreements arranged the boundaries of modern Kuwait, although Kuwait lost a significant amount of territory occupied by pro-Kuwaiti Bedouin to Saudi Arabia. A new boundary with Saudi Arabia was established, along with a Kuwait-Saudi Arabia Neutral Zone, an area of about 5,180 sq. km. (2,000 sq. mi.) which adjoined Kuwait's southern border. In December 1969, Kuwait and Saudi Arabia signed an agreement dividing the Neutral Zone (now called the Divided Zone) and demarcating a new international boundary. Both countries now share the Divided Zone's onshore and offshore petroleum equally.

The second challenge came from Iraq, which had emerged as an independent Arab state following British efforts to partition the Middle East after World War I and the collapse of the Ottoman Empire. As has been mentioned earlier, Iraq had no historical claim to Kuwait. Kuwait's northern border with Iraq had been established as part of the agreement Britain had reached with Turkey in 1913. Iraq accepted this claim when it was given its independence from Turkey, and accepted it again in the "Agreed Minutes between the State of Kuwait and the Republic of Iraq Regarding the Restoration of Friendly Relations, Recognition, and Related Matters," which Iraq and Kuwait signed in 1932. However, Iraqi nationalists began to claim Kuwait to be legitimately part of Iraq as early as the mid-1920s, and these claims laid the groundwork for later Iraqi claims and threats to Kuwait.

The third challenge was the discovery of oil in the 1930s, which began the transformation of Kuwait from a minor administrative port to a modern state. In 1938, however, a combination of the worldwide Depression, the collapse of the pearling industry and a Saudi trade boycott created a major economic crisis in Kuwait. Many leading merchants responded by challenging the authority of the Emir. They called for new arrangements that would share any wealth from Kuwait's new oil concessions, and a broader sharing of power by the Al Sabahs. The merchants first petitioned the Emir to achieve these goals, and then held unilateral elections for a Majlis. This body only lasted for six months before being suppressed by the Emir and other tribal leaders. However, its creation laid the ground work for a continuing Kuwaiti interest in representative government.

Modernization and Independence

The post war era saw Kuwait become a significant oil exporter. In 1950, Salim Al Sabah, a member of the Salim branch of the Al Sabah family, became Emir, replacing his predecessor, Ahmad al Jamir Al Sabah, who had ruled since 1921. Salim confronted the need to modernize and share Kuwait's growing oil wealth. During the 1950s, the new Emir created much of the welfare system which has given Kuwait some of the most advanced social services in the developing world. He also began a series of negotiations with Britain that replaced the treaty of 1899 with a treaty of friendship, which led to Kuwait's independence.

By the early 1960s, Kuwait began to move towards independence. In early 1962, the British withdrew their special court system, which handled the cases of foreigners residing in Kuwait, and the Kuwaiti Government began to exercise legal jurisdiction under new laws drawn up by an Egyptian jurist. Emir Salim responded to the fall of the Iraqi monarchy,

Iraqi threats to Kuwait, and threat of radical Arab socialism, by issuing Kuwait's first constitution in November, 1962. This constitution established the Emir as a hereditary monarch, as well as an Emir's Council, and a popular National Assembly whose electorate was limited to the descendants of Kuwait's population in 1920. The first election for the National Assembly took place in 1963.

Salim died in 1965, and was replaced by his brother Sabah who ruled Kuwait until December, 1977. Emir Sabah suspended the National Assembly in 1976, partly because of the deep divisions within the assembly, and partly because of its criticism of Iraq and other neighboring states. The National Assembly was allowed to operate again in 1981—largely in response to the fall of the Shah of Iran. The Assembly was suppressed again in 1986, however, because of its growing demands for power, its debates over a massive stock market fraud, charges of corruption involving the royal family, and debates that threatened to increase tension with Kuwait's neighbors.

Sheik Jabir al Ahmad al Jabir Al Sabah, a member of the Jabir branch of the Al Sabah family, became Emir in 1977, and continues to rule to this day. He has designated Prime Minister Saad al Abdullah as Salim Al Sabah as his successor—following a pattern in which the succession now alternates between the Jabir and Salim branches of the family. Sheik Jabir al Ahmad Al Sabah has been designated crown prince.

2

Kuwait's External Security: The Problem of Iran and Iraq

Kuwait enjoyed relatively peaceful relations with its neighbors until its independence in 1961. Saudi Arabia did not press its claims to disputed territory and offshore drilling areas as long as Kuwait remained under British protection. Iraq recognized Kuwait's independence in 1932 and did not challenge Kuwait's sovereignty while the Iraqi monarchy remained dependent upon British support and influence.

This situation changed dramatically after 1961. The Iraqi monarchy fell in 1958, and Kuwait faced a growing threat from radical Arab nationalism. The fall of the Iraqi monarchy had created a radical Iraqi regime which claimed Kuwait under the pretense that it had once been part of the Ottoman Empire and, consequently, was subject to Iraqi suzerainty. This threat was a major factor leading to Kuwait's decision to become fully independent on June 19, 1961.

Only a week after the withdrawal of British forces, Iraqi forces moved to the border. These forces only halted when Britain rushed troops back into Kuwait and it became clear that the Arab League was prepared to challenge Iraq's claims. Iraq signed an agreement in 1963 that appeared to recognize Kuwait's sovereignty, and the border demarcation to which Britain and Turkey had agreed in 1913, but Iraq only did so because of a coup that killed the Iraqi dictator who had originally threatened to invade Kuwait.

After this border crisis, Kuwait attempted to deal with external threats by adopting a policy of negotiation with any threatening power, and using its oil wealth to compensate for its military weakness. Kuwait gave money to the PLO and aid to radical Arab states. It provided funds to Syria and Iraq, supported Arab trade and oil embargoes, and terminated its treaty with Britain in 1971 in an effort to show it no longer had colonial ties. It bought military equipment from the US and Europe, but established relations with the Soviet Union in 1963, and eventually bought Soviet arms in an effort to minimize the risk of hostile Soviet pressure.

This policy of buying off threats helped Kuwait both to reach an agreement with Iraq in 1963, and get the votes it needed to join the UN. Nevertheless, Iraq continued to make sporadic claims to Kuwait, and never formally abandoned its claims to the Kuwaiti islands of Bubiyan and Warbah. These islands are on the northeastern edge of the Kuwaiti-Iraqi border. They control the Khor Abd Allah, the channel to Iraq's only means of direct access to the Gulf and its naval base at Umm Qasr, and are near its oil loading terminal in the Gulf off Al Faw.

Iraq threatened Kuwait again in 1965, 1967 and 1972. Iraq occupied Kuwait's border post at Samita on March 20, 1973, in a further effort to pressure Kuwait to cede its control of the islands in the Gulf. This led to the deployment of Saudi troops to the border. Iraq withdrew in early April, but only after mediation by Yasser Arafat and another substantial Kuwaiti payment to Iraq. Iraq then attempted to lease Warbah and half of Bubiyan in 1975 for a period of 99 years. According to some reports, Iraq briefly sent troops into Kuwait again in 1976, and only withdrew after another Kuwaiti payment.[5]

Kuwait and the Iran-Iraq War

Despite these difficulties, Kuwait was one of Iraq's most important allies during the Iran-Iraq War. During 1980–1988, Kuwait supplied Iraq with at least $13.2 billion in grants and loans, and with up to $22 billion in overall assistance.[6]

Even so, Kuwait's relations with Iraq continued to be problematic. Iraq again sought to lease Bubiyan and Warbah in 1980 and provoked another border incident in 1983. When Kuwait again refused to lease the two islands, Iraq sent a token force across the border. This Iraqi pressure led to a sudden visit to Baghdad by Kuwaiti Prime Minister Saad Sabah on November 10–13, 1984. Once again, Iraq was bought off by a substantial payment, although Iraq did establish a Hovercraft base across the river from Warbah.[7]

Control of Bubiyan and Warbah became steadily more important to Iraq during the early years of the Iran-Iraq War because Iraq could not secure its access to the Gulf through the Shatt al-Arab waterway, which it shared with Iran. The Shatt al-Arab suffered from eight years of silting and mining during the course of the Iran-Iraq War, and Iran demonstrated that its land-based anti-ship missiles could target any ships moving into Iraqi waters in the Gulf.

As a result, Iraq took steps to shift its shipping and naval operations as far south as possible. Iraq steadily expanded the southern commercial area of Basra, expanded the town of Al Zubayr, just to the southwest of Basra, and expanded its naval base at Umm Qasr. Iraq also moved south into territory that probably belonged to Kuwait near Umm Qasr and the border town of Safwan, and had expanded a canal called the Shatt al-Basra from Umm Qasr to a position midway between Basra and Al Zubayr. This made the Khor Abd Allah, the channel from the Gulf to Umm Qasr to the north of Bubyian and Warbah steadily more important.[8]

At the same time, Kuwait's support for Iraq created a threat from Iran. During 1980–1981, Iran conducted several overflights and air strikes on Kuwait to try to intimidate it into reducing its support for Iraq. Iran also attempted to gain support from Iranians living in Kuwait, and from Kuwaiti Shi'ites, which make up a substantial part of Kuwait's population.

These problems with Iran grew more severe after 1982, when Iranian forces drove Iraq out of Iran and began to counter-attack across the border into Iraq. It was clear to Iran's leadership that Kuwaiti aid played a critical role in giving Iraq the ability to survive Iranian attacks, and Iran began to put military pressure on Kuwait. While most of Kuwait's Shi'ite population proved loyal, Iran had some success in using Kuwaiti Shi'ites to attack targets in Kuwait.

On December 12, 1983, Shi'ites bombed the French and US embassies, and 17 Shi'ites were later convicted of the bombing. In May, 1985, pro-Iranian Shi'ites attempted to assassinate the Emir of Kuwait. Iran's conquest of Faw in 1986 brought it within striking distance of Kuwait. Pro-Iranian Shi'ites bombed Kuwait's oil facilities in June, 1986, and in January, April, May, and June of 1987. Iraq's increasing strikes on tanker and cargo traffic to Iran led Iran to retaliate by attacking tanker and cargo traffic to Kuwait and Saudi Arabia—creating a "tanker war" in the Gulf.

This "tanker war" led Kuwait to seek US and Soviet assistance in "reflagging" its tankers. Neither Kuwaiti military forces nor the GCC could provide the naval and air capabilities necessary to defend against the Iranian threat. Kuwait was forced to turn to the West and the USSR for aid. While the Soviet Union only provided token naval forces, the US provided a major naval escort effort, supported by US special forces and air units based in the Gulf. The escort effort led to significant naval clashes between the US and Iran during 1987 and 1988, which played a significant role in Iran's eventual defeat. It also led to the first major land-based anti-ship missile strikes on Gulf shipping. Iran fired at least 10 Silkworm missile at targets in Kuwaiti waters, forcing Kuwait to improve its navy and deploy countermeasure equipment on its islands.

Kuwait and the Gulf War

Iran's defeat in the Iran-Iraq War only created a new threat to Kuwait's security. Kuwait's support of Iraq during the Iran-Iraq War earned itself little gratitude. While Iraq emerged as the victor in the Iran-Iraq War, it had borrowed at least $37 billion in loans from Kuwait and its other Arab neighbors, as well as massive additional loans from the West and Japan. By late 1989, Iraq desperately needed to reschedule its debts. The required principal and interest on the non-Arab debt alone would have consumed half of Iraq's $13 billion worth of annual oil revenues.[9]

At the same time, repayments of this scale scarcely suited Saddam Hussein's growing regional ambitions. Iraq had a military budget of $12.9 billion in 1990, which meant Iraq was spending approximately $700 per citizen in a country with a per capita income of only $1,950.[10] As a result, Iraq began to demand forgiveness of its Arab loans during 1988 and 1989, and called for new grant aid to be given to Iraq as the sole defender of the Arab cause against Iran. Iraq also made new requests to lease Warbah and parts of Bubiyan island in 1989, and rejected the attempts of Kuwait's Emir to reach a general border settlement when he visited Iraq in September, 1989.[11]

By mid-1990, Iraq's cash reserves were only equal to three months of imports and inflation was running at 40%. When Kuwait refused to forgive Iraq's debt, lease the islands, and agree to Iraq's other border claims, Iraq decided on war. Saddam Hussein accused Kuwait of "stabbing Iraq in the back" and Iraqi foreign minister Tariq Aziz claimed that Kuwait had "implemented a plot to escalate the pace of gradual systematic advances towards Iraqi territory." He claimed that the Kuwaiti government had set up "military establishments, police posts, oil installations, and farms on Iraqi territory." He also claimed that Kuwait and the UAE were conspiring to keep oil prices low and were violating their oil quotas, and that Kuwait was stealing oil from the Rumalia oil field, whose southern tip enters Kuwaiti territory.[12]

On August 2, 1990, Iraq invaded a nearly defenseless Kuwait. It immediately became apparent that the GCC had no real military capability to aid Kuwait. The GCC had supposedly created a 10,000-man Peninsular Shield Force in the mid-1980s but, in reality, this force consisted of little more than a reinforced Saudi brigade based at Hafr al-Batin and token detachments from other Gulf states. Further, the so-called GCC rapid deployment force had little mobility and sustainability.

The US responded by forming the UN Coalition that fought the Gulf War and liberated Kuwait. However, Iraq's defeat has left a legacy of Iraqi irredentism, which has since been compounded by the impact of the UN cease-fire terms and the creation of a new border between Kuwait and Iraq.

When the UN Security Council accepted a cease-fire in the Gulf War on April 3, 1991, it adopted terms that required Iraq to (a) recognize the adjusted Kuwaiti-Iraqi border, (b) accept a UN guarantee of the border, (c) allow the UN to establish a peace observer force in a zone along the

Iraqi-Kuwait border 10 kilometers in Iraq and 5 kilometers in Kuwait, (d) reaffirm its commitment to the Chemical Warfare Convention and Nuclear Non-Proliferation Treaties, (e) permit the UN to ensure the destruction of all biological, chemical, and nuclear weapons, long-range ballistic missiles, and related facilities, equipment, supplies, (f) accept liability for Kuwait's losses, (g) assume liability for all pre-war debts, (h) return or account for all Kuwaiti prisoners, and (i) renounce terrorism. Iraq accepted these terms on April 4, 1991.

Kuwait and the Continuing Threat of Invasion from Iraq

Neither victory nor the cease-fire have ended the threat from Iraq, and Kuwait, the US, and other allied nations have repeatedly been forced to react to new Iraqi provocations. In August and September of 1992, the confrontation between Iraq and the UN over the elimination of weapons of mass destruction, and Iraq's treatment of its Shi'ites and Kurds, forced Kuwait and the US to transform their joint exercises into a demonstration that the US could protect Kuwait against any military adventures by Iraq. The US rushed Patriot batteries to both Kuwait and Bahrain, conducted a test pre-positioning exercise called Native Fury 92, deployed a 1,300 man battalion from the 1st Cavalry Division, and an amphibious reinforcement exercise called Eager Mace 92. The US also deployed 1,900 Marines and 2,400 soldiers, including two armored and two mechanized companies.[13]

Kuwait faces the prospect of continuing Iraqi challenges to its new border with Iraq. As part of the cease-fire terms, the UN set up a special UN Iraq/Kuwait Boundary Demarcation Commission. This commission issued its final report on May 20, 1993, and found that the original border marking points had long vanished, and that Iraqi farmers had steadily expanded their date farms to the south after the border was marked in 1923. As a result, correcting the border to the original line moved it to the north and into territory that Iraq had occupied before World War II.

The Secretary General accepted the final report of the UN Iraq/Kuwait Boundary Demarcation Commission, and the UN Security Council adopted Resolution 833 on May 27, 1993. Resolution 833 reaffirmed the Commission's final demarcation of the Iraq-Kuwait border, demanded that both states respect that border, and guaranteed the inviolability of the border.

The new border offered Kuwait considerable advantages at the expense of Iraq. It gave Kuwait greater control over the Ratga and Rumalia oil fields in its northern border area, and reduced Iraqi access to the port facilities at Umm Qasr.[14] At the same time, the new border created political problems with Iraq. Only six days after the Secretary General accepted the report, the Speaker of Iraq's National Assembly stated that the new border would keep tensions in the region high. Iraq refused to accept the new demarcation and Iraqi editorials, and Iran's media made new claims to Kuwait as Iraq's 19th province.

Iraq created a series of incidents in the border area during the rest of 1993 and through most of 1994. In late 1994, Iraq then sent major forces, including two Republican Guards divisions, into the border area. These movements forced the US to rush land and air forces into the area, and led to a new crisis between Iraq and the UN.

The continuing threat from Iraq became even more apparent on October 3, 1994, when Iraq began to move its Hammurabi and Al Nida Republican Guards divisions south from the area around Baghdad to positions about 20 kilometers from the border with Kuwait. These two units were the best equipped Republican Guards divisions in the Iraqi Army. They moved by rail and road with full ammunition loads and then deployed in an attack capable formation which had one brigade forward and two in the rear, and a full complement of divisional artillery.

The Iraqi movements not only involved two divisions of 9,000 to 10,000 men each, they involved the movement of FROG, SA-8, and mobile AA units. Iraq also increased the readiness of the Adnan and Baghdad divisions of the Republican Guards in the north in a manner that indicated they might move south, and altered the deployments of the three Iraqi divisions already in the south—the 54th Mechanized Division, which was about 40–50 kilometers from the border, the 2nd Armored Division, and the 4th Republican Guards Infantry Division. Iraq built up a total force of 70,000–80,000 men, which led to significant increases in the major weapons positioned in the area north of Kuwait. Iraqi tank strength increased from about 660 to 1,100, artillery strength from around 400 to 700, and OAFV strength from about 700 to 1,000.[15]

More than any incident since the Gulf War, this Iraqi build-up illustrated the problems Kuwait and the US face in dealing with a major Iraqi challenge and the necessary response. The Kuwaiti cabinet met in emergency session on October 7, 1994, and decided to send the Kuwait army to the border and put Kuwait forces on full alert. It took 5–7 days to deploy the Kuwaiti army fully, however, and its effective fighting strength was less than one heavy Iraqi Republican Guards brigade.

The US decided to send additional forces to the Gulf on October 9 to supplement the 13,000 US personnel already in the theater. These forces initially included the 18,000 men in the 1st Marine Expeditionary Force, 16,000 troops from the US army 24th Infantry Division, 306 fixed wing aircraft (including A-10s, F-16s, RF-4Cs, F-15Es, F-15Cs, F-111s, EF-111s, F-117s, JSTARS, F/A-18s, B-52s, and E-3As, 58 helicopters (including 54 AH-64s), two batteries of Patriot Missiles, and a carrier battle group. The US subsequently deployed another 73 fixed wing aircraft.

By October 12, the US had a total of 19,241 men in the Gulf area (1,923 Army, 11,171 Navy, 1,977 Marine, 3,844 Air Force, 173 Special Operations, and 153 Joint Task Force Headquarters). The US had two carrier task forces with 15 ships (counting one carrier battle group in the Red Sea) and 200 combat aircraft and was in the process of deploying significant numbers of aircraft.

US Army units were beginning to join the prepositioned US armor in Kuwait; and 5 Marine Corps Maritime Prepositioning Ships, 8 US Army Brigade Afloat Ships, and 6 USAF and US Army Prepositioning Ships were moving towards the Gulf. US forces were involved in joint exercises with Kuwaiti forces in the border area within a matter of days, and the US held a major, demonstrative armor–B-52-strike aircraft exercise before the end of October. In contrast, the Gulf Cooperation Council was only able to make a token commitment of the 17,000 man Peninsula Shield force—which lacked the combat capability to play any significant role in defending Kuwait.

Although Iraq backed down, withdrew its forces, and then stated it would recognize the new border with Kuwait, it seems clear that this Iraqi acceptance was little more than a ploy timed to try to put an end to UN sanctions. In fact, there were new indications of Iraqi movements against Kuwait in 1995. On August 8, 1995, two of Saddam Hussein's sons-in-law, two of his daughters, and other members of their family defected to Jordan. This defection was followed by unusual Iraqi movements around Baghdad and in Southern Iraq, and rumors that Iraq may attack Kuwait or make a demonstration near the border.

These indications led Kuwait to create a new security zone near its capital. At the same time, the US responded by deploying naval task forces where they could protect Kuwait as part of "Operation Vigilant Sentinel." On August 10, it alerted the carrier battle group that included the *Roosevelt* (CCG-8), the 8th Carrier Wing, the guided missile cruiser *Mississippi* (CGN), and the guided missile cruisers *Hue City* (CG) and *Ticonderoga* (CG), as well as the guided missile frigate *Nicholas* (FFG). This force was on station near Port Said by August 12, with the capability to launch more than 150 Tomahawk cruise missiles.

The US also alerted the 24th Marine Expeditionary Unit (MEU), the assault ships *Kearsarge* (LHD) and *Nashville* (LPD), and the guided missile destroyer *Burke* (DDG). The 11th Marine Expeditionary Unit (MEU) with the assault ships *New Orleans* (LPH) and *Juneau* (LPD), the landing ships *Comstock* and *Mt. Vernon* (LSD), and the TAO *Pecos*, moved from positions near the Gulf of Yemen to the upper Red Sea, where the MEU could rapidly deploy through Saudi Arabia. This force was also on station by August 12.

During all of this period, the carrier battle group in the new US 5th Fleet in the Gulf remained on station. This battle group included the carrier *Lincoln* (CCG-3), the 11th Carrier Wing, the guided missile cruisers *Vella Gulf, Princeton,* and *Chancellorsville* (CG), the guided missile destroyer *Jones* (DDG), the destroyers *Merill* and *Elliot* (DD), and the guided missile frigates *Ingraham* and *Stark* (FFG). The battle group in the 5th Fleet had the capability to deliver over 250 Tomahawks.

Kuwait and the US also decided to accelerate their joint exercises to take place in August rather than October. As a result, the US rushed some 28,000 troops to the region by mid-September, including 5,000 in the Eastern Mediterranean. It deployed 8 prepositioning ships from Diego Garcia to the Gulf, with enough gear to sustain 16,000 Marines in combat for 30 days, and 5,000–7,000 US Army troops. It deployed four additional prepositioning ships into the region. It also prepared US Army troops in the US for airlift to "marry up" with the heavy equipment for an armored brigade that is prepositioned at Camp Doha in Kuwait.

The US sent 1,400 troops to the exercise from the 1st Cavalry Division based at Fort Hood, Texas. It airlifted an advance guard of 398 soldiers to acclimate themselves, and check the prepositioned equipment, and then airlifted the remaining forces. These troops were deployed by August 17, and were soon conducting a month-long joint exercise called "Operation Intrinsic Action" with Kuwaiti forces near the border. Meanwhile, another 3,900 US Navy and Marine Corps force conducted a joint amphibious exercise with Kuwaiti forces called "Eager Mace 96-1." This exercise involved helicopter assault landings, live fire training, and surveillance operations.[16]

Kuwait and Lesser Threats from Iraq

Similar uncertainties regarding Iraq's future intentions exist as a result of a recent decline in Iraqi-provoked incidents along the border. Iraqi infiltrations and crossings dropped from several hundred a year during 1992–1994 to a few incidents a week in the spring of 1995. However, this decline seems to be a temporary tactic rather than a commitment to a lasting recognition of Kuwait's border.

Further, the decline in incidents is partly the result of the deportation of 1,500 Iraqis living in Umm Qasr (which occurred after Kuwait paid for new housing), and partly the result of improved border surveillance and the construction of a nearly 218 kilometer long security line. The border is now monitored by 300 unarmed observers from more than 30 countries, as well as a battalion of armed Bangladeshi soldiers The new security line has a three meter deep trench, followed by a five meter sand berm, and sensors which can detect the movement of vehicles. It is backed by a patrol road and outposts in the border area, and Kuwait is considering building a second defensive line behind it with mines and other barriers to halt an Iraqi military attack.[17]

It seems likely that Iraq will continue to assert its claims in the border area the moment it is given the political and military opportunity.[18] Kuwait has already had to abandon plans to allow Western oil companies to explore and develop its oil fields near the Iraqi border because of the risk of new clashes and incidents. Iraq, on the other hand, is aggressively attempting to negotiate deals with nations like Russia to exploit the fields on its side of the border once the UN sanctions are lifted.

Kuwait and Relations with Iran

Iraq is not the only external problem Kuwait faces. Iran threatened Kuwait several times during the Iran-Iraq War. It sent combat aircraft into Kuwaiti air space, deployed combat ships in Kuwaiti waters, and fired 10 anti-ship missiles at ships and port facilities in Kuwaiti waters. Iran also supported sabotage and terrorist attacks against targets in Kuwait. Iran still deploys land-based anti-ship missiles where they can cover shipping into all but Kuwait's most southern ports, and can rapidly deploy air, naval, mine warfare, unconventional warfare, and amphibious forces against Kuwait's islands, waters, and mainland.

Kuwait and Iran have never reached full agreement on their respective offshore oil and gas rights. Iran and Kuwait have discussed the issue, however, and there were reports that negotiations were underway in mid-1995. In dealing with Iran, Kuwait has also chosen dialogue over containment, and has done so with some success. It encouraged Iran to export to Kuwait, and imported $87 million worth of goods from Iran in 1994, versus exports of $6.6 million to $10 million. Kuwait has also taken measures to improve its relations with Iran by creating its first free-trade zone at Kuwait City's Shweikh port.[19]

Nevertheless, Kuwait cannot ignore the risk that Iran may become more threatening in the future. It may also find it difficult to fully exploit its offshore oil and gas resources as long as it is unable to reach a firm agreement with Iran or faces the threat of Iranian attacks on its offshore facilities.

Kuwait and Relations with Southern Gulf and Arab States

Kuwait's ruling family has kinship ties to the ruling family of Bahrain, but Kuwait has rarely taken sides in the quarrels of the other Southern Gulf states. It has concentrated on improving its own security and has encouraged efforts by the Gulf Cooperation Council to improve the defense of the Upper Gulf.

Kuwait has strongly encouraged GCC exercises in the Upper Gulf, and the growth of the GCC's Peninsular Shield force, although it has had little success in developing integrated GCC defenses in the area or combat-effective interoperable GCC forces which can defend against Iraqi heavy divisions. Kuwait has been effective, however, in getting strong GCC political support during the "tanker war" with Iran in 1987–1988, and during the Gulf War.

Kuwait's relations with Saudi Arabia have been the key to obtaining support in dealing with Iran and Iraq and have been relatively good since they signed a treaty in 1922. Kuwait and Saudi Arabia did argue occasionally over their respective rights to the neutral zone that had originally been established between them in order to give nomadic tribes freer access to grazing rights. However, they reached a agreement over this territory in 1966 and began to share the oil and gas resources in what they now called the "divided zone."

Saudi Arabia provided political support and troops to help Kuwait when Iraq threatened its border in the early 1960s. Saudi Arabia still did not recognize Kuwaiti sovereignty over all of Umm al-Maradem and Qaruh, however, and Saudi Arabia dealt with a dispute over offshore drilling rights by sending troops to occupy the two islands of Umm al-Maradem and Qaruh in June, 1977. Coupled to disputes with Iran, these tensions delayed Kuwait's full exploitation of its off shore oil resources.

Kuwait and Saudi cooperation improved after the fall of the Shah and the beginning of the Iran-Iraq War. Both nations began to cooperate more closely in dealing with Iran and in aiding Iraq. In 1990, Saudi Arabia played a key role in the liberation of Kuwait, and in July, 1995, they finally reached agreement over the demarcation of all their land and sea boundaries.[20] Kuwait and Saudi Arabia are now participating in joint exercises with the US in preparing for the defense of their borders against Iraq, and are expanding some aspects of this cooperation to include Bahrain.

In short, Kuwait's only significant problems with its neighbors stem from the inability of the GCC to emerge as an effective military alliance, the GCC's slow progress in developing effective, integrated defense capabilities with Saudi Arabia, and a feeling in much of the Southern Gulf that Kuwait is "arrogant" and "uncooperative"—a feeling that often seems to be more a reaction to Kuwait's wealth and focus on its own strategic concerns, rather than the result of any action on Kuwait's part.

Kuwait has close relations with most Arab states. It has been slow, however, to improve relations with Arab states that failed to support it during the Gulf War. Its relations with Jordan and Yemen have improved in recent years, but are still somewhat distant and Kuwait no longer provides either country with significant aid.

Kuwait has supported the Palestinian Authority in some aspects of the Arab-Israeli peace negotiations, but expelled many Jordanians and Palestinians from Kuwait after the Gulf War for sympathizing with Iraq. Many Kuwaitis bitterly resent what they perceive as Jordanian and Palestinian betrayal of Kuwait, and Kuwait has sharply reduced the number of foreign Arab workers in Kuwait. It has been cautious in reaching out to Israel, but relations are relatively friendly.

3

Political and Economic
Stability and Security

The recent trends in the Kuwaiti economy are shown in Table One. The longer term trends are summarized in Chart One and Chart Two. Table One shows the impact of the Gulf War, Kuwait's subsequent recovery, its dependence on oil exports and revenues, and its acute dependence on the government budget for virtually every aspect of its economic activity. The oil sector continues to provide more than 80% of all Kuwaiti government revenues.[21]

Chart One shows an estimate of the trends in Kuwait's GDP relative to population and per capita income in constant 1987 dollars. Chart Two shows an estimate of the trends in Kuwait's GDP, central government expenditures, military expenditures, total exports, and arms imports as measured in constant 1993 US dollars. While these charts are complex, they provide a clear picture of the truly devastating impact of Iraq's invasion on Kuwait's GDP and exports, and show the massive increases Kuwait had to make in central government expenditures and military expenditures to cope with the costs of the war. This expenditure was in excess of $66 billion and cut Kuwait's reserve "Fund for Future Generations" from nearly $100 billion to around $35 billion.[22]

Kuwait had to pay these costs after a long period of relatively low oil prices, which substantially cut Kuwaiti revenues during much of the 1980s. Chart One shows the World Bank estimates that Kuwait's GDP per capita dropped by an average of 0.8% per year during 1979–1989.[23] This is a significant cut, although it is much smaller than the drop in GDP per capita in most Southern Gulf states during this period. Kuwait was partially able to compensate for low oil prices by investments in downstream and upstream operations and other activities.

At the same time, Chart One and Chart Two show that Kuwait recovered relatively quickly from the impact of the war. Similarly, the CIA estimates that Kuwait's GDP had recovered to the point where it had a purchasing power equivalent of $30.7 billion in 1994. Petroleum and

TABLE ONE Key Economic Indicators in Kuwait

EIU Estimate*	1990[a]	1991[b]	1992	1993	1994	1995
Production (1,000s of barrels per day)	1,937	460	1,060	1,690	1,870	2,043
Oil Exports (1,000s of barrels per day)	1,850	370	1,035	1,794	1,905	1,923
Average Oil Export Price (per barrel)	14.55	—	—	14.07	13.48	15.36
Oil Export Receipts ($US current billions)	6.3	0.86	6.22	10.00	11.18	—
GDP ($US current billions)	18.16	10.81	18.82	23.65	24.24	—
Per Capita GDP ($US current)	8,527	5,222	13,434	16,538	13,245	—
Total Government Revenue ($US current billions)	7.634	2.234	8.055	9.199	8.860	9.812
Total Government Expenditures ($US current billions)	12.144	21.128	14.255	14.980	14.794	15.244
Budget Balance ($US current billions)	-4.51	-18.89	-6.20	-5.78	-5.93	-.543

Middle East Economic Digest Estimate**	1994	1995	1996
Population (Millions)	1.83	1.96	2.07
Native Kuwaitis	0.68	0.71	0.75
GDP ($US current billions)	24.3	25.3	25.5
Annual GDP Growth (percent)	1.1	4.0	1.0
Inflation (percent)	3.0	4.5	4.0
Unemployment (percent)	0.5	0.5	0.7
Total Foreign Debt ($US current billions)	10.98	9.6	8.2

(continues)

TABLE ONE *(continued)*

*Middle East Economic Digest Estimate***	*1994*	*1995*	*1996*
Exports ($US current billions)	11.15	12.0	12.25
Imports ($US current billions)	6.64	7.0	7.1
Trade Balance ($US current billions)	4.52	5.0	5.15
Current Account ($US current billions)	2.99	2.34	1.20

Notes: ªJanuary–July.
bSeptember–December.
cIncludes crude oil, oil products, and LPG.
Source: Adapted by Wayne A. Larsen, NSSP, Georgetown University, from the EIU, Country Profile, *Kuwait, 1995–1996*, pp. 10, 11, 17, 27–31.
**Source:* Adapted by Anthony H. Cordesman from *Middle East Economic Digest*, February 23, 1996, p. 8.

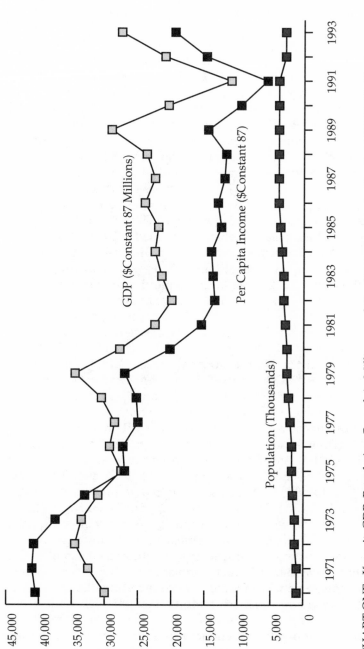

CHART ONE Kuwait: GDP, Population Growth in Millions, and Per Capita Income (in Constant $87 US Dollars).
Source: Adapted by Anthony H. Cordesman from International Energy Agency (IEA), *Middle East Oil and Gas*, Paris, 1995, pp. 305–309.

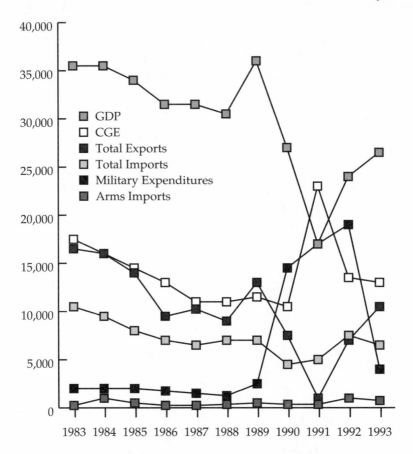

CHART TWO   Kuwaiti Gross Domestic Product, Central Government
Expenditures, Military Expenditures, Total Imports, Total Exports, and Arms
Deliveries: 1983–1993 (in Constant $93 US Millions). *Source:* Adapted by
Anthony H. Cordesman from ACDA, *World Military Expenditures and Arms
Transfers, 1993–1994,* ACDA/GPO, Washington, 1995.

petrochemicals accounted for over 50% of Kuwait's GDP and 90% of its
exports and government revenues. Kuwait's only other major industries
were desalination, salt, food processing and construction. Aside from a
small fishing industry, agriculture accounted for well under 0.1% of
Kuwait's GDP, and Kuwait imported over 96% of its food. Kuwait's foreign debt totaled roughly $7.2 billion. Kuwait had only 525 cubic meters
of freshwater per capita, and over 75% of its potable water had to be dis-
tilled or imported.[24]

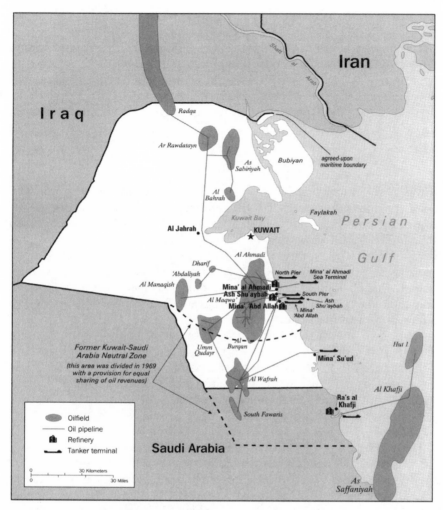

MAP TWO   Kuwaiti Energy Facilities

Kuwait's economy underwent a further recovery in 1995. It had largely rebuilt its prewar ability to exploit its massive oil and gas resources. In spite of major drawdowns in foreign investment holdings to pay for the Gulf War, Kuwait also managed to retain a major pool of investments to help meet both its current funding needs and to provide income in the future. Kuwait was also making significant new investments in downstream industries.

Kuwait rivals the UAE for the title of the wealthiest Gulf state in terms of total savings and oil and gas resources per capita. As a result, it does not face the same near and mid-term economic constraints as most of its Southern Gulf neighbors. Kuwait does, however, face limits on its financial resources. It used up a significant portion of its investment capital during the Gulf War, and is still experiencing budget deficits that constrain what its government can spend on defense, social services, and development. Like the other Southern Gulf states, Kuwait also faces the need to reduce its dependence on foreign labor and encourage a more productive private sector.

Kuwait's Oil Industry

Kuwait's oil industry is the core of its national wealth and economy. The US Department of Energy (DOE) estimates that Kuwait is one of the largest oil powers in the world. According to the DOE, Kuwait has an estimated 94 billion barrels of recoverable oil, or 9.4 percent of the world's total. The Neutral Zone or Divided Zone area, which Kuwait shares with Saudi Arabia, holds an additional 5 billion barrels of reserves, half of which belong to Kuwait. Kuwait also has gas reserves of 52.4 trillion cubic feet (about 1.1% of the world total), and produces about 93.5 billion cubic feet of gas per year.[25]

Table Two shows that the US Department of Energy estimates that Kuwait will steadily increase in importance as a world oil producer, and will produce 3.0–4.0 millions of barrels per day by the early 2000s. These goals are close to those set by Kuwait, which seeks a production capacity of 3.3 millions of barrels per day by 2000, and 3.8 millions of barrels per day by 2005—including 0.3 millions of barrels per day from the Neutral Zone.[26]

Table Three and Chart Three show an International Energy Agency (IEA) estimate of Kuwait's share of Gulf and world oil reserves and oil production. These data further reinforce Kuwait's strategic importance as a major holder of oil reserves and oil producer. It is important to note that Kuwait's reserves rank very close to those of Iran and Iraq, and that the data on Kuwait reserves may well be more reliable.

Kuwait provides a slightly higher estimate of its proven oil reserves. It estimates that it has 96.5 billion barrels of proven reserves, which it calculates are 9.6% of the world total. Kuwait estimates that it has over 100 years of reserves at its current production rate of 2.06 million barrels per day, but any such estimates are theoretical because there has never been a comprehensive seismic survey of its reserves. Two and three dimensional surveys are now underway in Kuwait's onshore and offshore fields and the Neutral Zone, but will not be complete until around the year 2000.[27]

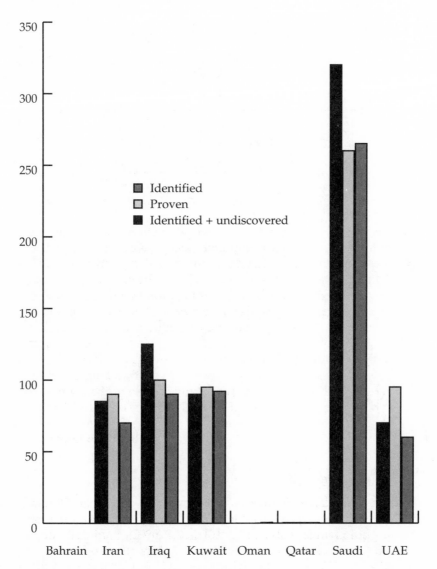

CHART THREE   Total Oil Reserves of the Gulf States (in Billions of Barrels).
Source: IEA, *Middle East Oil and Gas,* Paris, OECD, IEA, Annex 2, and data
provided by Bahrain and Oman. Bahrain's reserves are only 350 million barrels
and do not show up on the chart because of scale.

TABLE TWO   Estimated Increase in World Oil Production by Region and Country

Country/Region	1990	1992	2000 Base Case	2000 Range	2005 Base Case	2005 Range	2010 Base Case	2010 Range
OPEC	27.8	27.2	37.5	35.0–41.8	42.1	36.8–45.5	46.5	39.2–49.1
Middle East & Gulf								
Iran	3.2	3.6	4.3	4.2–4.7	5.0	4.5–5.4	5.4	4.9–5.7
Iraq	2.2	0.4	4.4	4.0–5.1	5.4	4.6–6.0	6.4	5.5–6.6
Kuwait	1.7	1.1	2.9	2.8–3.2	3.6	3.1–3.9	4.2	3.5–4.6
Qatar	0.5	0.4	0.6	0.5–0.7	0.6	0.5–0.7	0.6	0.5–0.6
Saudi Arabia	8.5	9.6	11.5	10.8–12.5	12.8	11.5–13.5	14.1	12.3–14.6
UAE	2.5	2.6	3.1	2.9–3.3	3.5	3.0–3.7	4.3	3.3–4.5
Total Gulf	18.6	17.7	26.8	25.2–29.52	30.9	27.2–33.2	35.0	30.0–36.6
Algeria	1.4	1.3	1.5	1.4–1.8	1.3	1.0–1.5	1.1	0.7–1.3
Libya	1.6	1.6	1.8	1.6–2.2	2.1	1.8–2.3	2.0	1.2–2.2
Total Middle East	21.6	20.6	30.0	—	34.3	—	38.0	—
Total OECD	20.1	20.6	20.3	18.4–21.5	19.7	16.6–21.1	19.4	15.5–21.1
US	9.7	9.7	8.2	7.3–8.6	8.2	6.6–8.9	8.6	6.4–9.5
North Sea	4.2	4.6	5.3	4.9–5.6	4.6	4.2–4.8	4.2	3.7–4.4
FSU**	11.5	9.1	7.8	7.3–8.5	9.4	8.3–10.7	10.9	9.2–11.5
Eastern Europe	0.3	0.2	0.2	0.2–0.3	0.2	0.1–0.2	0.2	0.1–0.2
Asia								
China	2.8	2.8	3.1	2.9–3.4	3.4	3.0–3.6	3.2	2.7–3.4
Indonesia	1.5	1.7	1.4	1.2–1.5	1.1	0.9–1.3	1.0	0.7–1.2
Australia	0.7	0.6	0.7	0.5–0.8	0.6	0.4–0.7	0.5	0.3–0.6
Other Asia	1.7	1.7	2.1	1.9–2.4	2.1	1.7–2.3	1.8	1.4–2.0

(continues)

TABLE TWO (continued)

Country/Region	1990	1992	2000 Base Case	2000 Range	2005 Base Case	2005 Range	2010 Base Case	2010 Range
Latin America								
Venezuela	2.6	2.6	3.3	3.0–3.7	3.8	3.4–4.1	4.3	3.6–4.5
Mexico	3.0	3.1	3.2	3.0–3.4	3.3	2.9–3.5	3.3	2.8–3.5
Other	2.2	2.4	3.5	3.2–3.9	3.3	2.9–3.5	3.1	2.7–3.3
Sub-Saharan Africa								
Gabon	0.3	0.3	0.3	0.3–0.4	0.3	0.2–0.3	0.2	0.2–0.3
Nigeria	1.8	2.0	2.4	2.3–2.7	2.6	2.3–2.8	2.8	2.4–3.0
Other	1.8	1.9	2.1	1.8–2.5	2.0	1.5–2.2	1.9	1.4–2.1
World Total	69.6	67.4	78.6	72.5–86.6	84.2	72.6–91.4	88.8	73.7–94.7

*Less Syria and Egypt.
**Former Soviet Union.

Source: Adapted by Anthony H. Cordesman from EIA, *International Energy Outlook, 1995*, Washington, DOE/EIA-048(95), p. 29. The EIA, Oil Market Simulation Model Spreadsheet, 1994, data provided by the EIA Energy Markets and Contingency Information Division, and EIA, *International Energy Outlook, 1994*, pp. 11–20.

TABLE THREE Comparative Oil Reserves and Production Levels of the Gulf States

Comparative Oil Reserves in 1994 in Billions of Barrels

Country	Identified	Undiscovered	Identified and Undiscovered	Proven	% of World Total
Bahrain	—	—	—	.35	8.9
Iran	69.2	19.0	88.2	89.3	10.0
Iraq	90.8	35.0	125.8	100.0	9.7
Kuwait	92.6	3.0	95.6	96.5	NA
Oman	—	—	—	5.0	0.4
Qatar	3.9	0	3.9	3.7	26.1
Saudi Arabia	265.5	51.0	316.5	261.2	9.8
UAE	61.1	4.2	65.3	98.1	64.9
Total	583.0	112.2	695.2	654.1	35.1
Rest of World	—	—	—	345.7	100.0
World	—	—	—	999.8	

(continues)

TABLE THREE (continued)

Comparative Oil Production in Millions of Barrels per Day

Country	1995 Actual	OPEC Quota	DOE/IEA Estimate of Actual Production 1990	1992	2000	2005	2010	Maximum Sustainable 1995	2000	Announced Capacity in 2000
Bahrain	—	—	—	—	—	—	—	—	—	—
Iran	3,608	3,600	3.2	3.6	4.3	5.0	5.4	3.2	4.5	4.5
Iraq	600	400	2.2	0.4	4.4	5.4	6.6	2.5	5.0	5.0
Kuwait	1,850	2,000	1.7	1.1	2.9	3.6	4.2	2.8	3.3	3.3
Oman	—	—	—	—	—	—	—	—	—	—
Qatar	449	378	0.5	0.4	0.6	0.6	0.6	0.5	0.6	0.6
Saudi Arabia	8,018	8,000	8.5	9.6	11.5	12.8	14.1	10.3	11.1	11.1
UAE	2,193	2,161	2.5	2.6	3.1	3.5	4.3	3.0	3.8	3.2
Total Gulf	—	—	18.6	17.7	26.8	30.9	35.0	23.5	28.2	28.2
World	—	—	69.6	67.4	78.6	84.2	88.8	—	—	—

Source: Adapted by Anthony H. Cordesman from estimates in IEA, *Middle East Oil and Gas*, Paris, OED/IEA, 1995, Annex 2 and DOE/EIA, *International Energy Outlook, 1995*, Washington, DOE/EIA, June, 1995, pp. 26–30, and *Middle East Economic Digest*, February 23, 1996, p. 3. IEA and DOE do not provide country breakouts for Bahrain and Oman. Reserve data estimated by author based on country data.

Most of Kuwait's oil reserves are located in the 65 billion barrel Greater Burgan area, southeast of Kuwait City. This productive area contains the Burgan, Magwa, and Ahmadi fields. The Raudhatain (6–7.5 billion barrels of reserves), Sabriya (3.8–4.0 billion barrels of reserves), and Minagish fields (2–2.1 billion barrels of reserves) are located in northern Kuwait. All of these fields have been producing since the 1950s, and generally contain heavy to medium crude oil with gravities in the 30 to 36° API range. Two additional large oil fields were discovered in 1984, although their reserves still are unproven. The South Magwa field contains light crude oil with a 35 to 40° API. The other field, located in northern Kuwait, contains heavy crude oil.[28]

Kuwait has five fields in the Neutral Zone, which it shares with Saudi Arabia. These include Khafji, with 6.3 billion barrels of reserves, Wafra, with 1.7 billion barrels of reserves, South Umm Gudair Wafra, with 0.45 billion barrels of reserves, Hout with 0.2 billion barrels of reserves, and South Fuwaris, with 0.04 billion barrels of reserves. Kuwait also shares the Ratga oil field with Iraq.

Kuwaiti Oil Production

Kuwait has no petroleum law; the Emir of Kuwait, Sheik Jaber al-Ahmed al-Sabah, has ultimate authority over all major decisions relating to oil. The Sheik's principal advisor is the Oil Minister. A Supreme Petroleum Council was established in 1974 to review all major decisions. This Council is chaired by the Foreign Minister. Its membership includes six other ministers, and members of the private sector appointed by the Emir.

Kuwait nationalized all domestic and foreign oil assets on December 1, 1975, and created the Kuwait Petroleum Company (KPC) in 1975. It is an umbrella company for domestic and international subsidiaries that handle exploration, pipelines, engineering, refining, marketing, petrochemicals, tankers, aviation fuel, and the refining and marketing of products for Kuwait's retail outlets.

The oil produced in the Kuwait-Saudi Neutral Zone is shared equally between the two countries. The KPC owns a 10% share in the Arabian Oil Company that operates offshore production in the zone, while Saudi Arabia Texaco operates the onshore production.

Chart Four shows the trends in Kuwaiti oil production. Kuwait had produced a total of about 27 billion barrels of oil at the time of the Iraqi invasion in August, 1990, and had an extremely high reserve-to-production ratio of 194/1.[29] Kuwaiti oil production peaked in 1974 at 2.94 million barrels per day. Kuwait produced oil at a rate of about 1.0–1.9 million barrels per day during 1990, and was producing at 1.9 millions of barrels per day just before the Iraqi invasion. Including the Kuwaiti share of the

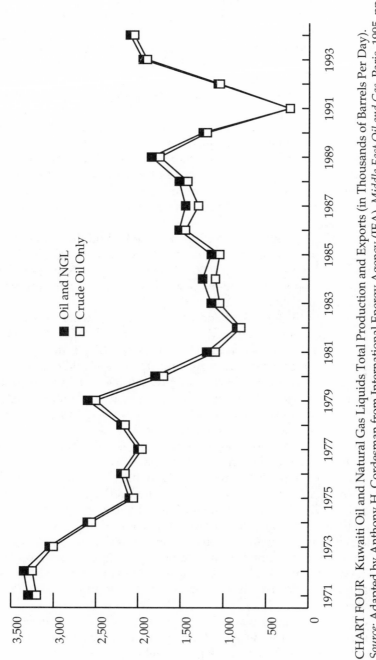

CHART FOUR Kuwaiti Oil and Natural Gas Liquids Total Production and Exports (in Thousands of Barrels Per Day).
Source: Adapted by Anthony H. Cordesman from International Energy Agency (IEA), *Middle East Oil and Gas,* Paris, 1995, pp. 252–256.

Neutral Zone, Kuwait had a sustainable production capacity of 2.3 millions of barrels per day, and was operating a total of 898 wells.[30]

When Iraq retreated in 1991, it used explosives on over 700 wells and set about 600 on fire and another 49 gushing—creating oil lakes. Iraq damaged or destroyed all 26 of Kuwait's oil gathering centers. Kuwait has since estimated that this damage cost it up to 3% of its recoverable reserves, although there is no way to make precise estimates and this damage is still under study.[31]

Kuwait began reconstruction soon after the cease-fire, and phase one continued until the end of 1991. Well fires were extinguished some nine months after the liberation and contracts were let to work over the old wells and drill new ones. Contracts were let for the recovery of crude oil from Kuwait's oil lakes, and about 17 million barrels were recovered from lakes totaling around 20 million barrels. This phase of reconstruction cost about $2.5 billion.

Phase Two of the reconstruction effort included rebuilding wells, gathering centers, pipelines, storage tanks, refineries, and terminals. As of 1995, Kuwait had returned 18 of its 26 oil gathering centers to operation, with a capacity of about 2.8 millions of barrels per day. It had reworked over 650 wells and drilled 111 new ones.

Phase Three is still underway and calls for the expansion of Kuwaiti oil, gas, and petrochemical production, and creating a total of 30 oil gathering centers. Its total cost is estimated at four to six billion dollars.[32]

Production has recovered relatively rapidly since the liberation.[33] In mid-1993, Kuwait's oil output surpassed pre-war levels. In 1994, Kuwait produced an estimated 2.04 millions of barrels per day, including 360,000 barrels per day of Neutral Zone production. Kuwait's 1995 production capacity is estimated at 2.6 million barrels per day.

While Kuwaiti oil exports to the United States have been relatively small, they have expanded from 40,000 barrels a day before the Gulf War to around 240,000. Kuwait has restored its status as one of the world's few oil powers that can serve as a major swing producer in the event of an emergency. The US Department of Energy (DOE) estimates that Kuwait and Saudi Arabia hold roughly 80 percent of the world's excess production capacity.[34] Other estimates also indicate that Kuwait faces relatively low total capital costs in maintaining and expanding its oil production capacity. These data are shown in Table Four, but it should be noted that they may sharply understate indirect costs and the full impact of recent expansion plans.

The DOE also estimates that Kuwait's rapid postwar boost in oil production has resulted in some short-term problems. An increased proportion of water has been lifted in relation to oil at a number of wells. For example, water cut at the 1.5-million barrels per day Burgan field rose

TABLE FOUR   Cost of Maintaining and Expanding Oil Production in GCC
             Countries (1993–2000) (in Billion of CY93 US Dollars)

Country	Cost of Maintaining Capacity	Cost of Expanding Capacity	Total Cost
Kuwait	3.40	3.00	6.40
Qatar	0.84	0.60	1.44
Saudi Arabia	11.2	6.90	18.10
UAE	4.00	2.40	6.40
Total	19.44	12.90	32.34

Source: The NCB Economist, Issue No. 4, May, 1993, issued by the National Commercial Bank of Saudi Arabia as quoted by Yousef H. Al-Ebraheem in a draft paper for the National Defense University.

from 8 percent before the war to 25 percent in 1994. This increase, however, may be due to the rise in the number of periphery wells used in reservoir management programs. In 1993, the state-owned Kuwait Oil Company (KOC) commissioned country-wide reservoir simulation studies. The Minagish and Zubair field studies reported damage resulting from well blowouts at the Minagish and Zubair fields. Studies on Burgan, Umm Gudair, and other fields have completion dates in mid-1995.[35]

Kuwait has three major export terminals on the Gulf coast near its refineries at Mina al Ahmadi, Mina Abdullah, and Shuaiba, and had a fourth in the Neutral Zone at Mina Saud that was destroyed during the Gulf War. These three terminals were damaged during the war, but the commercial port at Shuaiba opened in March, 1991, and oil shipment resumed in 1992. The total export capability of Kuwait's terminals is now about 2.9 million barrels per day, and Kuwait is planning to add two single point mooring buoys. Oil storage capacity has been returned to its 16 million barrel pre-war level.

Plans to Expand Production

Kuwait plans to steadily raise its oil production. This increase in production plays a major role in most estimates of the increases in world oil exports necessary to support global economic growth and development. Kuwait plans to raise its crude oil production, excluding the Neutral Zone, to 3 million barrels per day by the year 2000 and 3.3–3.5 million barrels per day by 2005. This will involve a number of new projects in western and northern Kuwait.[36]

Kuwait's financial difficulties and contract delays put several projects on hold in 1994, but progress picked up in early 1995. Kuwait's expansion program will include the installation of gas/oil separation plants, gas compression facilities, desalting plants, and enhanced oil recovery systems at several fields. Also, an injection plant is under construction to provide pressure maintenance at the Minagish and Raudhatain fields. In March, 1995, the China Petroleum Engineering Construction Corporation signed a $390 to $430 million contract to build two crude oil gathering centers in the western 2 billion barrel Minagish and Umm Gaidar fields. Output from the fields will be raised from 110,000 barrels per day at present to 500,000 barrels per day in 1997. These fields will be linked by pipeline to the Mina al-Ahmadi refinery.[37]

Kuwait is also undertaking development work at the northern 250,000-barrels per day Raudhatain, 130,000 barrels per day Sabriya, and 35,000 barrels per day-combined Ratga and Abduliya fields. In 1992, British Petroleum (BP) signed a three-year technical service contract to work on the Minagish and Umm Gaidar fields. In February, 1995, this contract was extended to include technical support at the Raudhatain and Sabriya fields. In August 1994, Chevron signed a technical service agreement similar to BP's according to which it would provide exploration, production, and transportation assistance to KOC's Burgan field's operations.

Kuwait is seeking to boost capacity through the construction of gathering centers in its western fields at Umm Gudair and Minagish. It awarded the China Petroleum Corporation a $390 million contract in December, 1995 to lift capacity from 110,000 barrels per day to 500,000 barrels per day.[38]

These BP and Chevron contracts are important evidence of Kuwait's increasing willingness to allow greater foreign upstream involvement. In February, 1995, the Kuwait Petroleum Company (KPC) decided to offer PSCs to foreign companies. Kuwait stated that the reasons for this decision included technology transfer and a greater perceived international interest in Kuwait's territorial integrity. In June, 1995, however, Kuwait decided to delay such plans because it concluded that the risk of new clashes with Iraq offset the possible advantages to be gained from foreign involvement in Iraqi-border area oil field development in ensuring foreign support in the event of another crisis with Iraq.[39]

As of May, 1995, KPC's PSC proposal was still awaiting final approval from the Supreme Petroleum Council. If passed, a limited number of companies would be asked to bid for a share of the work. They might include Amoco, BP, Chevron, Exxon, Mobil, Occidental, Royal Dutch/Shell, and Texaco. These firms are particularly interested in offshore PSCs, which have better perceived development prospects.

Kuwait is also cooperating with Saudi Arabia in expanding production from the "Divided" or "Partitioned Neutral Zone" shared by the two countries. Texaco and Japan's Arabian Oil Company (AOC) are the two foreign operators of the 400,000 barrels per day Neutral Zone shared by Kuwait and Saudi Arabia. In March, 1995, Texaco received permission to boost its current production of 140,000 barrels per day to almost 300,000 barrels per day by 1998. This will be accomplished through new drilling and a 3-D seismic survey to discover new reserves. Most work is expected to occur at the South Umm Gaidar, Wafra, and South Fawaris fields.

Kuwait is rumored to have given Texaco the development contract partly because of the company's ability to market heavier crude oil. As of April, 1995, the AOC was continuing negotiations concerning concession extensions for its 300,000 barrels per day offshore production. Currently, AOC's Neutral Zone concessions expire in 2000 and 2003, respectively. AOC is holding off on further investment until these dates are extended.[40]

Downstream and Upstream Investments

Kuwait operates three refineries at Mina al Ahmadi, Mina Abdullah, and Shuaiba, and has a share in the refinery at Mina Saud in the Neutral Zone. Kuwait's refining capacity was damaged severely during the war and the Mina Saud and Shuaiba refineries were badly damaged. Kuwait lost much of its pre-war, 770,000 barrels per day capacity, and only had 200,000 barrels per day of refinery output by early 1992. However, Kuwait's $400 million downstream reconstruction program was completed in mid-1994. Mina al Ahmadi went from 370,000 barrels per day pre-war throughput capacity to 390,000, Mina Abdullah boosted capacity from 190,000 to 225,000, and Shuaiba increased from 187,000 to 144,000. Mina Saud is not operating. KPC is now focusing increasingly on high-value product exports, which rose 83 percent to 642,000 barrels per day between 1993 to 1994.[41]

In May, 1995, KPC initiated a new program to complete final, small repairs and to begin refinery upgrades. The 200,000 barrels per day Shuaiba refinery suffered the most damage from the war. At present, capacity has been raised to 144,000 barrels per day. The new repair program will work on restoring the 65,000 barrels per day processing unit as well as upgrading the 20,000-barrels per day hydrocracker's second stage. Completion of the Shuaiba repairs is anticipated by 1997. The 390,000 barrels per day Mina al-Ahmadi refinery upgrade will involve the construction of three units to produce unleaded gasoline for domestic consumption. The $100 million contract was awarded to Mitsui and will be completed by 1998. Similar upgrading will take place at the smaller 225,000-barrels per day Mina al-Abdullah refinery.

Kuwait now plans to achieve a domestic refinery capacity of 900,000–1,000,000 barrels per day by 2000. It is not seeking to expand its domestic capacity much beyond this level, but hopes to shift its refinery output to more valuable product streams. It also plans to expand its ownership of foreign refineries to ensure it has guaranteed markets.[42]

KPC is expanding its overseas downstream interests in the hope of attaining a combined European and Asian refining capacity of 835,000 barrels per day by 2000. It is currently seeking 300,000 barrels per day of refining capacity in Europe and 400,000 barrels per day in Asia.

In May 1995, two agreements with the state-owned Indian Oil Company (IOC) and Cochin Refineries Limited (CRL) were pending. The IOC deal involves a new $1.3 billion, 125,000 barrels per day refinery in Orissa, India. Depending on demand this proposed refinery's capacity may be raised to 180,000 barrels per day. The proposed CRL Indian refinery would be located in Kerala and would have a capacity of between 120,000 to 200,000 barrels per day.[43]

Kuwait Petroleum International (KPI) controls the country's European refinery system. This includes 130,000 to 150,000 barrels per day in capacity from refineries in Gulfhaven, Denmark and Rotterdam in the Netherlands. Kuwait is looking to expand its European refinery system through the acquisition of an Italian refinery, possibly the under-used 300,000 barrels per day refinery in Sardinia. KPI is also pursuing talks with Italy's Agip concerning the possibility of acquiring its 300,000 barrels per day refinery in Milazzo, Sicily. Since 1993, KPI has been searching for a replacement for its antiquated 100,000-barrels per day Naples refinery after it failed to meet Italy's environmental standards.

In February, 1995, KPC undertook a feasibility study concerning a possible 90,000 barrels per day refinery near Karachi, Pakistan. Also, a 300,000 barrel per day refinery in Rayong, Thailand, is under discussion, as well as a possible export refinery located near Pattaya on Thailand's southern coast. In South Africa, KPC is currently negotiating with Sasol to acquire part of its 85,000 barrels per day Natref refinery. KPC hopes this acquisition would secure a market for its present 25,000 barrels per day worth of crude oil exports to South Africa.

Kuwait is also expanding its investments in petrochemicals. It has been producing fertilizer since the mid-1960s, and had just started building a major complex at Shuaiba when the war began. In mid-1993, Kuwait's state-owned Petrochemical Industries Company (PIC) and Union Carbide Corporation formed a joint venture to build and operate a world-scale petrochemical complex at Shuaiba. Construction of the $2.3-billion facility began in late 1995, and the plant is due to be completed in 1997. PIC and Union Carbide each have a 45 percent share in the project, with the remainder reserved for public offer. The complex will include a 650,000 metric ton per year (mt/y) ethane cracker, 450,000 mt/y of polyethylene capacity, and 350,000 mt/y of ethylene glycol production. After its completion in 1997, the complex will primarily serve

Asian products markets. Kuwait is also negotiating with US Amoco Corporation to build a $1 billion aromatics plant.[44]

KPC also holds Santa Fe Exploration, which has production shares in five UK sector North Sea oil fields. Santa Fe Exploration also holds an 8.5 percent stake in the giant Britannia gas field. Britannia is expected to come on-stream in late 1996 with an output of 600 million cubic feet per day and 50,000 barrels per day of condensate. After startup, Santa Fe Exploration will produce an estimated 14,000 barrels per day. Kufpec is another foreign upstream asset owned by KPC. In 1994, it had an annual production of roughly 15,000 barrels per day from operations in Australia, China, the Congo, Egypt, Indonesia, and Tunisia. Kufpec's production is predicted to double during 1995 after two new oil fields in Yemen come on-line.[45]

Kuwait has, however, been forced to sell a large share of its international investments in foreign upstream operations. Part of these sales have gone to pay for budget deficits, and part to pay for the Gulf War. Part occurred because the assets were not as profitable as Kuwait originally expected. For example, in November, 1994, Kuwait announced its intention to sell Santa Fe International's US subsidiary—Santa Fe Minerals—which conducts exploration and production in North and South America. KPC had originally purchased Santa Fe in 1981 for $2.5 billion. During the 1980s, this subsidiary lost an estimated $3 billion.[46]

Kuwaiti Gas Reserves and Production

Table Five, Table Six, and Chart Five show that Kuwait ranks among the twenty nation's with the world's largest gas reserves, although its reserves are not large by Gulf standards. Kuwait estimates that it has 1.5 trillion cubic meters, or 1.1% of the world's reserves.[47] All of Kuwait's gas reserves are associated with oil fields, and all of its natural gas production is carried out by the Kuwait Production Company.

Kuwait has established gas gathering facilities and pipelines, but its efforts to find separate gas fields have failed. As a result, the gas production shown in Chart Six has varied with oil production—a trend reflected in the decline in gas production during 1980–1985 and the massive drop in production resulting from Iraq's invasion.

Chart Six shows that Kuwait made progress in utilizing its gas for domestic needs and oil production purposes before the Iraqi invasion. The share of Kuwait gas that was marketed rose from 42% in 1975 to 74% in 1989, but massive amounts had to be flared during the first phase of the Gulf War.

The Kuwait gas industry suffered some war damage. Three of Kuwait's five gas booster stations were damaged, and one was destroyed. However, its LPG plant and bottling unit were not damaged. Gas production and domestic use has since recovered, but Kuwait actually needs more

TABLE FIVE   World Natural Gas Proven Reserves by Country as of January 1, 1995 (Trillion Cubic Feet)

Country	Reserves	Percent of World Total
World Total	4,980.3	100.0
Top 20 Countries	4,595.8	92.3
Former Soviet Union	1,977.0	39.7
Iran	741.6	14.9
Qatar	250.0	5.0
Abu Dhabi	188.4	3.8
Saudi Arabia	185.4	3.7
United States	162.4	3.3
Venezuela	130.4	2.6
Algeria	128.0	2.6
Nigeria	120.0	2.4
Iraq	109.5	2.2
Canada	79.2	1.6
Norway	70.9	1.4
Mexico	69.7	1.4
Malaysia	68.0	1.4
Netherlands	66.2	1.3
Indonesia	64.4	1.3
China	59.0	1.2
Kuwait	52.4	1.1
Libya	45.8	0.9
Pakistan	27.5	0.6
Rest of World	384.5	7.7

Note: The sum of the shares for the top 20 countries may not equal their total share due to independent rounding.

Source: Worldwide Look at Reserves and Production, *Oil and Gas Journal,* Vol. 92, No. 52 (December 26, 1994), pp. 42–43.

gas than it produces, and was an importer from Iraq before the war. Kuwait is now looking for other sources of gas.

Kuwait's Economy Since the Gulf War

As the previous tables have shown, Kuwait's post war recovery has been relatively rapid. Kuwait was able to restore most of its urban services as early as mid-1991. Despite some apocalyptic predictions, the 732 oil well fires Iraq set during its withdrawal did not produce fatal environmental problems, and all were extinguished by the end of October, 1991. Kuwait was able to resume oil exports, and exported one million barrels per day by mid-1992.

TABLE SIX   Gulf and Gas Reserves and Production

	Reserves in 1995		Percent World	Production in
Nation	TCF	BCM	Supply	1993 (BCM)
Bahrain	—	—	—	—
Iran	741.6	21,000	14.9	60.0
Iraq	109.5	3,100	2.2	2.75
Kuwait	52.9	1,498	1.1	5.17
Oman	600–640			
Qatar	250.0	7,070	5.0	18.4
Saudi Arabia	185.9	5,134	4.2	67.3
UAE	208.7	5,779*	4.2	31.63
Gulf	1,548.6	—	31.1	185.25
Rest of World	3,431.7	104,642	68.9	—
World Total	4,980.3	148,223	100.0	—

Note: *Other sources estimate 6,320–7,280 BCM for Abu Dhabi only.

Source: The reserve and production data are adapted by Anthony H. Cordesman from IEA, *Middle East Oil and Gas,* Paris, OECD, IEA, 1995, Annex 2.

Table One has already shown that Kuwait's short term balance of trade is favorable, and other sources indicate that Kuwait has had a favorable trade balance during the last few years—with a surplus of $4.0 billion in 1993, $5.0 billion in 1994, $2.35 billion in 1995, and an estimated surplus of $2.10 billion in 1996. In 1994, Kuwait had approximately $11.8 billion worth of exports.[48]

Chart Seven shows the longer term trends in Kuwait's balance of trade. It shows that Kuwaiti oil exports have averaged over 2 million barrels a day since August, 1993, and Kuwaiti oil revenues grew from $5.9 billion in 1992 to $9.3 billion in 1993, and an estimated $10.3 billion in 1994. In spite of the war and some financing problems, the Kuwaiti GDP grew by over 22% in 1993, and 13% in 1994. This gave Kuwait a GDP equivalent of about $30 billion in 1994, total reserves of about 11 billion Kuwaiti dinars, and a per capita income of over $20,000 a year.[49]

Kuwait does, however, face significant problems in reducing its level of government spending and in restructuring its economy. Chart One has shown that Kuwait's real per capita income has dropped steadily since the late 1970s for other reasons—largely the decline in oil prices and rise in Kuwait's population. This chart is a warning that even the wealthiest state must take careful account of the vulnerability inherent in having a commodity-dependent economy and rapid population growth.

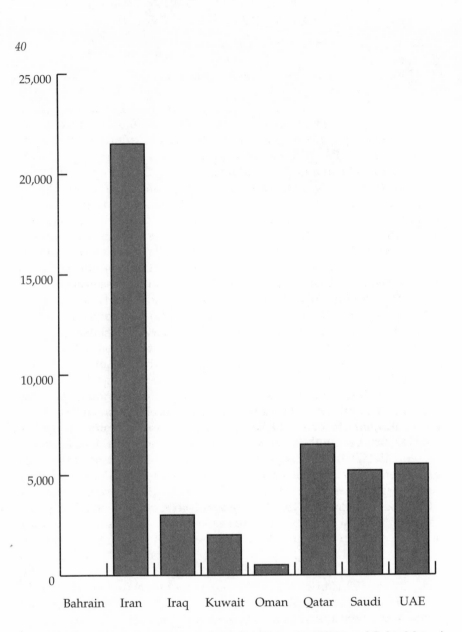

CHART FIVE   Total Gas Reserves of the Gulf States (in Billions of Cubic Meters).
Source: Adapted by Anthony H. Cordesman from IEA, *Middle East Oil and Gas,*
Paris, OECD, IEA, 1995, Annex 2, and data provided by Bahrain and Oman.
Bahrain's reserves are too small to show on the chart because of scale.

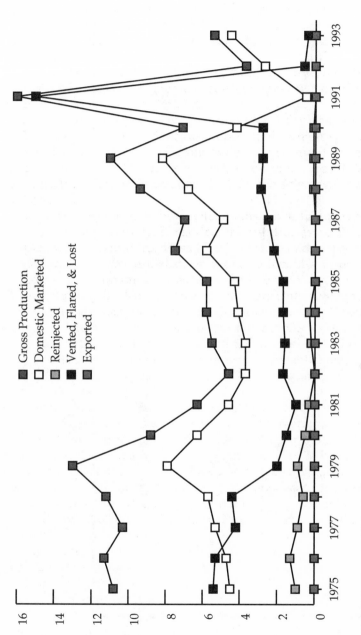

CHART SIX Kuwaiti Natural Gas Production (in Billions of Cubic Meters). *Source:* Adapted by Anthony H. Cordesman from International Energy Agency (IEA), *Middle East Oil and Gas,* Paris, 1995, pp. 252–256.

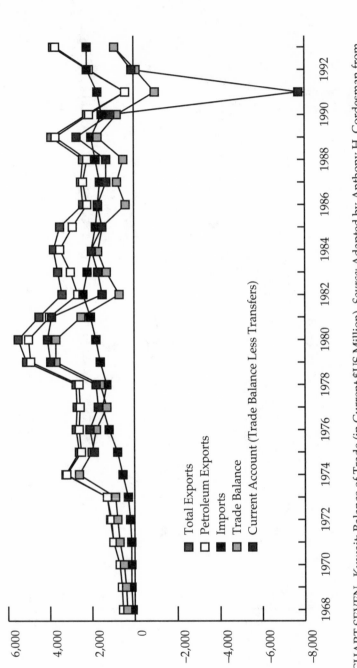

CHART SEVEN Kuwait: Balance of Trade (in Current $US Million). *Source:* Adapted by Anthony H. Cordesman from International Energy Agency (IEA), *Middle East Oil and Gas*, Paris, 1995, pp. 274–275, Central Bank of Kuwait, *Quarterly Statistical Bulletin.*

Kuwait's Budget, Liquidity, and Debt

In spite of Kuwait's oil wealth, the Kuwaiti government spends far more than it receives by way of revenues. Table Seven shows that the government established a pattern of deficit spending long before the Gulf War, and that its total revenues only exceeded its expenditures during one year in the period between FY1984/85 and 1995/96.

These deficits were relatively unimportant before the Gulf War because they did not fully reflect income from Kuwait's foreign investments. The Kuwait government, however, was forced to make massive expenditures during the Gulf War. Table Seven shows, however, that the government had to make massive direct expenditures to cope with Iraq's invasion of Kuwait, the struggle to liberate Kuwait, and wartime damage to the Kuwaiti economy. It shows that Kuwait's deficits totaled over 14 billion Kuwaiti Dinars ($48 billion) in the three years following the invasion, and that Kuwait's average deficit has exceeded one billion Kuwaiti Dinars in every year since FY1992/93. Further, the reduction in Kuwait's deficits from FY1994/1995 onwards has been largely the result of the fact that Kuwait assumed oil prices of $12 a barrel in FY1994/1995 and $13 a barrel in FY1995/1996, and world prices rose to higher levels. Even then, the rise in oil prices scarcely ended Kuwait's deficits. A significant peak in oil prices in late 1995 and early 1996 was only estimated to have reduced Kuwait's 1996 deficit from 1.3 billion Dinars to 1.0 billion Dinars ($3.32 billion).[50]

The budget data in Table Seven also understate the true level of government spending. Many of Kuwait's expenditures to pay for the Gulf War are "off budget" in the estimates shown in Table Seven. According to one estimate, Kuwait had to draw heavily on its Fund for Future Generations, which totaled up to $100 billion before the war, to help fund the liberation. Kuwait pledged up to $65 billion of this total to pay for the Gulf War—nearly 65% of the total assets it had invested. Kuwait then had to obligate some $20 billion for repairs and modernization of its oil facilities, make massive arms purchases to rebuild its military forces. It then had to pay $20 billion more to repay bad loans stemming from the collapse of Kuwait's unregulated curb-side stock market—or Souq al-Manakh—in 1982.[51] Another estimate indicates Kuwait spent $49 billion during the first seven months of the invasion, a total of $66.7 billion by the end of FY1994/1995, and that this expenditure depleted Kuwait's total government-held foreign investments by at least 40%.[52]

Chart Eight and Chart Nine show the longer trends in Kuwait's budgets and confirm the importance of budget reduction and fiscal controls. They show the impact of changing oil prices after the early 1980s, and the massive impact the Gulf War had on Kuwait's deficit,

TABLE SEVEN Kuwaiti Budget Revenues and Expenditures Relative to Earnings: 1984–1996 (Millions of Kuwaiti Dinars)

Trend: FY1984/1985 to FY 1995/1996[53]

Fiscal Year	Oil Revenues	Other Receipts	Total Revenue	Total Expenditures	Deficit
1995/1996	2,490	420	2,910	4,230	1,320
1994/1995	2,243	402	2,637	4,140	1,503
1993/1994	2,324	451	2,775	4,241	1,466
1992/1993	2,085	278	2,364	3,937	1,573
1991/1992	496	151	647	6,112	5,462
1990/1991	246	27	273	7,619	7,346
1989/1990	2,936	299	3,235	3,096	–139
1988/1989	2,035	333	2,368	2,999	631
1987/1988	1,991	260	2,252	2,806	554
1986/1987	1,484	247	1,731	2,860	1,129
1985/1986	2,095	250	2,345	3,106	761
1984/1985	2,494	251	2,745	3,205	460

Spending by Category: FY 1993/1994 to FY 1995/1996

	93/94 Approved Budget	93/94 Closing Account	94/95 Approved Budget	94/95 Budget After Additional Allocation	95/96 Approved Budget
Revenues					
Oil Revenue	2,419.8	2,324.3	2,234.9	2,234.9	2,490.0
Other Receipts	293.9	450.8	402.3	402.3	420.0
Total Revenues	2,713.7	2,775.1	2,637.2	2,637.2	2,910.0
Expenditures					
Wages & Salaries	1,160.0	1,003.5	1,144.0	1,144.0	1,164.5
Goods & Services	276.0	248.8	263.0	303.0	261.0
Transport & Equipment	45.0	34.7	35.0	35.0	30.0
Development Projects	345.0	400.4	340.0	408.4	379.5
Miscellaneous Expenditure/Transfers	2,111.0	2,553.4	2,358.0	2,482.3	2,395.0
Total Expenditure	3.937.0	4,240.8	4,140.0	4,372.7	4,230.0
Net Deficit	1,224.0	1,465.7	1,502.8	1,735.5	1,320.0

Source: Adapted from the *Middle East Economic Digest*, September 1, 1995, p. 6 and February 23, 1996, p. 10; and Central Bank of Kuwait and Ministry of Finance.

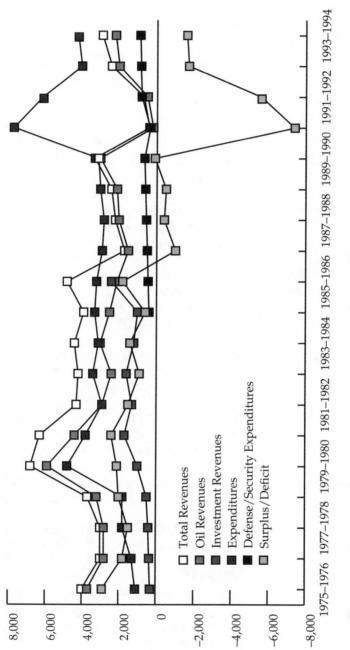

CHART EIGHT Trends in Kuwait Budget Revenues and Expenditures (in Millions of Kuwaiti Dinars). *Source:* Adapted by Anthony H. Cordesman from International Energy Agency (IEA), *Middle East Oil and Gas,* Paris, IEA/OECD, 1995, pp. 277–278.

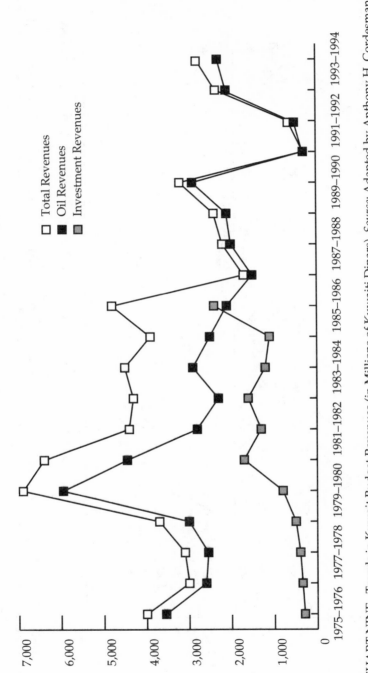

CHART NINE Trends in Kuwait Budget Revenues (in Millions of Kuwaiti Dinars). *Source:* Adapted by Anthony H. Cordesman from International Energy Agency (IEA), *Middle East Oil and Gas*, Paris, IEA/OECD, 1995, pp. 277–278.

oil earnings, and earnings from investments. They show that Kuwait's revenues have recovered sharply since the war, but that Kuwait has continued to experience financial pressure because of its large reconstruction costs and debts. During 1991–1993, it also faced major new defense costs, a loss of investment revenue, and low oil prices. These factors led to a deficit of $18 billion out of total spending of $21 billion in 1992.

The Kuwaiti budget deficit reached a wartime peak of about 7.3 billion Kuwaiti Dinars in 1990/1991, and then dropped to 5.5 billion in 1992/1993, 1.6 billion in 1993/1994, and 1.5 billion in 1994/1995. At the same time, Kuwait faced sudden emergency defense expenditures, like $500 million in costs to deal with the Iraqi movement to positions near the Kuwait border in October 1994.[54] The government's fiscal debt levels also increased, and deficit spending reached $6.2 billion out of total government expenditures of $15.4 billion in 1994/5—with only limited reductions projected for 1995/96.[55]

Some of Kuwait's deficit spending has gone into productive capital investments like rebuilding the country and investing in oil and gas facilities, but much continues to go to subsidies and welfare. Kuwait has no direct taxation, and Kuwait's Finance Ministry has stated that the country spends about $1.8 billion a year on utility subsidies and free health care alone. In 1994, the Kuwaiti government was still subsidizing 90% of all electricity costs and 75% of all water costs, and still providing low-cost telecommunications, free health care, and free housing. It was spending $1 billion a year on subsidizing water and power, and $600 million on subsidizing health care.[56]

These subsidies made little sense in a country as wealthy as Kuwait, and led the Kuwaiti government to consider various economic austerity measures in 1994—many of which were similar to those being considered or adopted by other Gulf states. The government examined the possibility of cuts in government subsidies and welfare benefits, increases in taxes, privatization of state-owned enterprises, and banking sector reforms, selling electricity and water at market prices, privatizing telecommunications and charging market prices, indirect taxation, and requiring some degree of private health insurance.

It soon became apparent, however, that the government faced major practical and political problems in implementing any such measures. There were many areas where it could not achieve immediate savings because of the cost of reform. For example, charging for services like utilities involved installing utility metering capabilities for the first time. It also ran into major political problems. Conservatives argued that most Kuwaitis were too poor to pay higher taxes and that income disclosures violate personal privacy.

Most importantly, Kuwait's next parliamentary elections are scheduled for October, 1996 so few members of the National Assembly have any incentive to push for major fiscal reform before the election. As a result, the Kuwaiti government continues to temporize, and Kuwait continues to use the capital it obtains from selling foreign investments and borrowing to pay for recovery from the war and support its social benefits.

These factors led Kuwait to raise its debt ceiling from $10 billion to $33 billion after the Gulf War, and borrow $5.5 billion from international banks. Kuwait also drew down on its foreign investments to finance the country's high public spending levels. Chart Ten shows that Kuwait retained substantial liquidity in spite of these expenditures, but estimates differ. The US government estimated in early 1995 that Kuwait had total reserves of roughly $61 billion, with $23.2 billion in its General Reserve and $40–45 billion in the Reserve Fund for Future Generations.[57] A Kuwaiti estimate made in early 1996 indicates that Kuwait's total foreign investments dropped from $113 billion (34 billion Kuwaiti Dinars) before the war to $46.7 billion (14 billion Kuwaiti Dinars), and that the Kuwaiti government was forced to reduce its foreign investments by an average of $500–750 million a month during 1993–1996.[58]

Chart Eleven shows that the sectoral structure of Kuwait's GDP is less dependent on oil than that of most Southern Gulf states. Kuwait's postwar investments and reserves, however, are very different from their pre-Gulf War total of over $100 billion. Kuwait's external debt has risen to $9.4 billion.[59] Kuwait also owes a $5.5 billion syndicated loan to foreign banks which must be paid by the end of 1996, and owes other small amounts to official export credit agencies (ECA). According to Kuwaiti government officials, these obligations will be paid on schedule and according to terms. Kuwait paid $2.486 billion in 1995, and this payment will increase to $3.298 billion in 1996.[60]

Kuwait has, however, solved one long-standing debt problem. The collapse of the Souq al-Manakh in 1982 created some $20 billion in losses and massive debt payments for stocks bought on margin. A "difficult debts law" was passed in 1993 to schedule repayment of these debts, and Kuwaiti private investors faced the prospect of repaying about $8.3 billion (2,300 million Kuwait dinars) by September 7, 1995, as part of this legislation. After extended debate in the National Assembly, the government passed legislation that allowed repayment in five annual payments beginning on December 6, 1995. This solution could have cost the economy up to $2.6 billion because of the delay in payments. Fortunately for the government, 75% of debtors paid the amount they owed by December, 1995.[61]

Much now depends on Kuwait's ability to increase oil production and the level of future oil revenues. Higher oil prices did improve

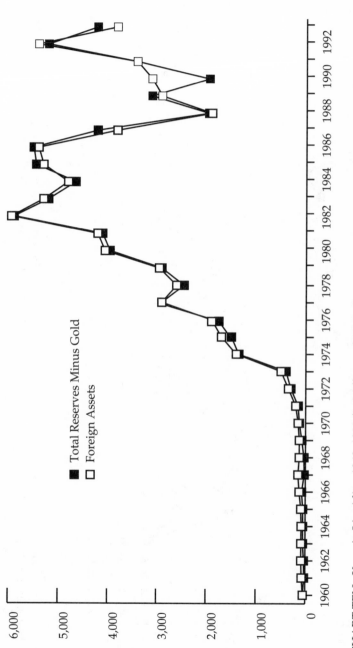

CHART TEN Kuwait: Liquidity: 1960–1993 (in Millions of US Dollars). *Note:* No data on foreign assets after 1992.
Source: Adapted by Anthony H. Cordesman from International Energy Agency (IEA), *Middle East Oil and Gas,* Paris, 1995, pp. 277–279, and based on IMF, *International Financial Statistics.*

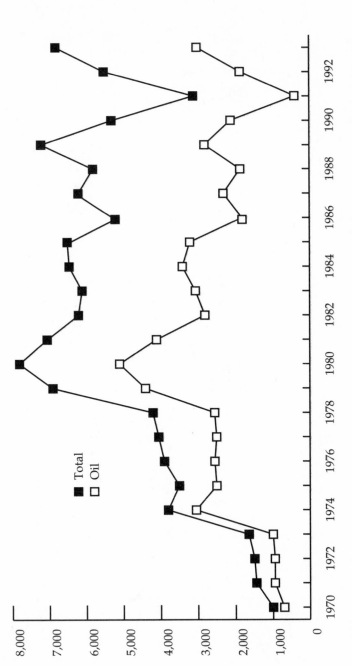

CHART ELEVEN Kuwait: GDP by Sector (in Millions of Kuwaiti Dinars). *Source:* Adapted by Anthony H. Cordesman from International Energy Agency (IEA), *Middle East Oil and Gas,* Paris, 1995, pp. 265–266, Central Bank of Kuwait, *Quarterly Statistical Bulletin.*

Kuwait's economic position in 1994 and 1995. Some estimates indicate that Kuwait's oil revenues increased by 12–14% in 1995.[62] If oil prices remain relatively high, and government expenditures are controlled, Kuwait's debt situation should ease and the economy should grow significantly in 1996.

At the same time, higher oil revenues cannot eliminate the government's need to show fiscal restraint and support for economic reforms. As long as the government fails to take firm action, and the National Assembly blocks tax and revenue reform, Kuwait will emphasize welfare over development and security and will have to draw still further on its general reserves.[63]

The Need to Create Real Jobs for Native Kuwaitis

Kuwait does not have the same population and economic pressures as the other Southern Gulf states, but it needs to seriously consider its future as a society and how its citizens will play a role in its future economy. Kuwait needs to create an economy that offers its citizens real job opportunities and reduces its dependence on foreign labor. It also needs to create a large, productive private sector, in addition to its state controlled oil and gas industries and service industries.

Chart Twelve shows that a conservative World Bank estimate projects that Kuwait's population will grow from 15.9 million in 1995, to 18.8 million by the year 2000, 2.1 million by 2005, 2.3 million by 2010, and 2.6 million by 2020. About 40% of Kuwait's native population is now under 14 years of age. The total number of young men reaching job age (15–19 years) will rise from 83,000 in 1995 to 117,000 in 2000, drop to 111,000 in 2010, and then rise to 114,000 in 2020.[64] Kuwaiti estimates indicate that 55% of Kuwait's population is under 19, and that 6,000 to 10,000 more Kuwaiti males will enter the labor force each year for the next 10–15 years.

Even today, far too many Kuwaitis lack productive jobs and real careers. Petroleum still accounts for nearly half of Kuwait's GDP and about 88% of its export and government revenues. Kuwait's only industries other than petroleum-related activity and desalinization are food processing, building materials, salt, and construction. The government controls nearly 90% of Kuwait's economy—either directly or through controls on large-scale commercial operations.

Further, nearly 92% of all employed Kuwaiti citizens either work for the government or a government-owned enterprise, and the state sector makes up about 63% of total government employment. The cost of government personnel totalled roughly $6.7 billion (2.0 billion Kuwaiti Dinars) a year.[65] In spite of government policies that supposedly encour-

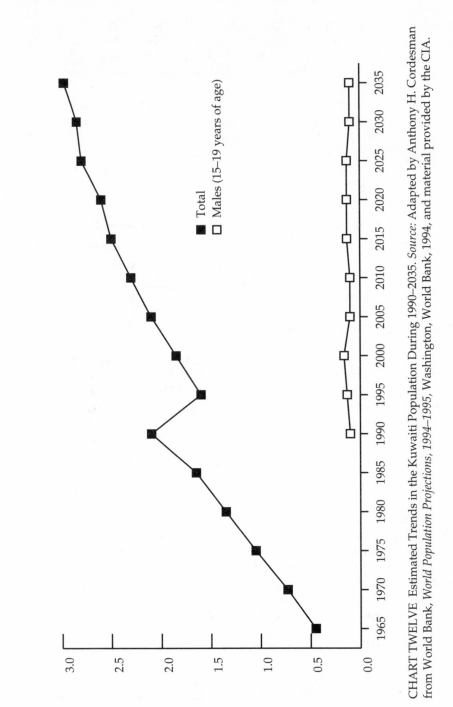

CHART TWELVE Estimated Trends in the Kuwaiti Population During 1990–2035. *Source:* Adapted by Anthony H. Cordesman from World Bank, *World Population Projections, 1994–1995,* Washington, World Bank, 1994, and material provided by the CIA.

age limitations on the government funded work force, the number of Kuwaitis directly employed in government increased from 168,000 in 1988 to 248,000 in 1994.[66]

While no accurate figures are available on the sectoral distribution of Kuwait's labor force, World Bank estimates indicate that 74% of Kuwait's labor force works in service jobs (including government, government-owned firms, and the military), 24.7% in industry (including oil), and 1.3% in agriculture (including fishing).[67]

There are less than 10,000 Kuwaitis employed in the private sector. In contrast, the number of expatriate workers in Kuwait has increased from 1.4 million in 1990, before the Gulf War, to 1.83 million in 1994.[68] This increase has taken place in spite of Kuwaiti discussion about reducing its dependence on foreign labor after the Gulf War, and the expulsion of Palestinians, Jordanians, and Bidoon. The net result has been to "de-Arabize" Kuwait by importing more Asian workers, and foreign workers now make up 83% of the total work force and 99% of the work force in the private sector.[69]

This reliance on government employment is extraordinarily costly to both Kuwait's economy and its society. Kuwaiti ministers and intellectuals may disagree on many issues, but not over the fact that the government employs four to five Kuwaitis for every real job. Further, there is an equal consensus over the fact that most employed Kuwaitis do little more than interfere with each other's efforts or complicate the operations of an already cumbersome and inefficient government sector. As a result, there are far more employed Kuwaitis that reduce the net output of the economy than increase it. Roughly 80% of all employed Kuwaitis have no economic function of any kind; their jobs are meaningless and a net liability to the nation.

These problems are compounded by a lack of incentives to take real jobs or be productive, and an educational system that does little to prepare most Kuwaiti nationals for a productive role in the private sector—either educating them in areas with few job prospects or over-educating them for the jobs available.

Kuwait's cradle-to-grave welfare society has provided free medical care, generous gifts and loans to defray the cost of weddings, funerals and free housing. It offers forgiveness for most mis-investments in Kuwait's "camel market," a house, interest free loans, free education through graduation from college, and guaranteed employment after graduation from college.[70] It has not, however, provided a path towards development or social cohesion based on social purpose.

In order for Kuwait to develop a more productive distribution of labor, it will have to shift native labor into industry and more productive service jobs. Over 96% percent of Kuwait's food is imported, and much of the fishing and agricultural activity that does take place only does so because of non-economic government subsidies. Small amounts of local vegetables are grown by farmers receiving such subsidies, and limited amounts are sold to neighboring countries. However, far too few vegetables are grown to have any significant impact in meeting local food needs, and virtually no agricultural production would take place if Kuwait did not provide subsidies and low-cost water.[71]

These changes, however, require aggressive privatization measures, and ones which emphasize speed and scale over social equity. The Kuwaiti National Assembly is correct in pointing out that there is little point in privatization which creates private monopolies as a substitute for existing government monopolies. The end result of such measures might simply be to cut jobs as the new owner made an operation more efficient, while transferring profits from government to private hands. At the same time, efforts to limit the size of individual investments and prevent the sale of operating entities to the private sector could sharply reduce entrepreneurial and competitive activity, and the incentive for outside investment. Kuwait lacks suitable anti-trust and anti-monopoly legislation, and suitable commissions to manage utility industries and regulate anti-trust activity.[72]

Kuwait does not need instant privatization, but it does need to act quickly and decisively and to shatter the "welfare ethic" that applies as much to Kuwaiti investment as to government services. Kuwait also needs far more joint ventures like the $2 billion petrochemical plant it is building as a joint venture between the Kuwaiti Petrochemical Industries Corporation and Union Carbide, and to take the risk of offering foreign oil companies acreage for exploration and development.[73]

The Need for Structural Reform

Per capita oil and investment wealth are relative—even in a nation with as many oil reserves as Kuwait. Some estimates indicate that Kuwait's native population will nearly double between 1995 and 2020. If such estimates are even approximately correct, Kuwait needs the kind of structural economic reform that will allow privatization to create new jobs and industries, and reduce its dependence on foreign labor.[74] It needs to offer real career opportunities to both its current citizens and many of its "foreign" workers and permanent residents like its Bidoon. Kuwait also needs to face the reality that population growth is likely to reduce per capita oil wealth even if oil prices remain at current or higher levels and production increases.

These needs are recognized in a World Bank report issued in 1993, which was published in Kuwait's local English press. This report advocated an economic program that would reduce the deficit, privatize many government-owned companies and services, reduce subsidies and promote employment of Kuwaiti citizens in the private sector. The US State Department reports that most Kuwaiti officials agree with the overall conclusions of the report, but that little has been done to date to move toward specific implementation of the report's recommendations. As a result, a number of Kuwaiti and foreign experts believe that the changes listed below are required in the Kuwaiti government's structural policies. Kuwait needs to:

- Reduce dependence on welfare, and reserve subsidies only for its poor citizens. Water, electricity, motor gasoline, basic foods, and many services need to be priced at market levels and subsidies to citizens need to be replaced with jobs and economic opportunities.
- Force radical reductions in the number of foreign workers, with priority for reductions in servants and in trades that allow the most rapid conversion to native labor. Charge high fees for foreign labor permits and force all foreign labor to pay not only the cost of all government services, but pay a premium over cost.
- Force social changes in Kuwait by eliminating guaranteed employment in the government and ensuring that government salaries lag sharply behind those in the private sector. Kuwait's young and well-educated population needs to be given jobs, and Kuwaiti society must adapt to the reality that its present dependence on foreign labor is a major threat to Kuwait's national identity and security.
- Educate Kuwaitis to regard government jobs as having low status and to understand that most government jobs are now a net liability to the Kuwaiti economy. Freeze and then reduce the number of civil servants. Restructure and down-size the civil service to focus on productive areas of activity with a much smaller pool of manpower. Cut back sharply on state employees by the year 2000.
- Restructure the educational system to focus on job training and competitiveness. Create strong new incentives for faculty and students to focus on job-related education, sharply down-size other forms of educational funding and activity, and eliminate high overhead educational activities without economic benefits.
- Eliminate economic disincentives for employers hiring native labor, and create disincentives for hiring foreign labor.
- Shift all government impacted goods and services to market prices. Remove distortions in the economy and underpricing of water, oil, and gas.
- Implement extensive privatization to increase the efficiency of Kuwaiti investments in downstream and upstream operations. Cre-

ate real jobs and career opportunities for native Kuwaitis, and open investment opportunities up to a much wider range of investors. Kuwait has already begun this process but it needs to be sharply accelerated to remove productive activity from government control. At the same time, privatization must be managed in ways that ensure all Kuwaitis an opportunity to share in the privatization process. It should not be conducted in a way that benefits only a small elite group of investors and discourages popular confidence and willingness to invest in Kuwait.

- Stop subsidizing Kuwaiti businesses in ways which prevent realistic economic growth and development, and which deprive the government of revenue. Present policies strongly favor Kuwaiti citizens and Kuwaiti-owned companies. Income taxes are only levied on foreign corporations and foreign interests in Kuwaiti corporations, at rates that may range as high as 55 percent of net income.

- Tax earnings and sales with progressive taxes that reduce or eliminate budget deficits, encourage local investment, and create strong disincentives for the expatriation of capital, including all foreign holdings of capital and property by members of elite and ruling families. This will provide a key source of revenue, and make the distribution of income more equitable. Kuwait needs to ensure that wealthier Kuwaiti's make a proper contribution to social services and defense.

- Allow foreign investment on more competitive terms. Kuwait currently allows foreign investment in limited sectors of the economy, in minority partnerships, and on terms compatible with continued Kuwaiti control of all basic economic activities. Some sectors of the economy—including oil, banking, insurance and real estate—have traditionally been closed to foreign investment. Foreigners (with the exception of nationals from some GCC states) are not permitted to trade in Kuwaiti stocks on the Kuwaiti Stock Exchange, except through the medium of unit trusts. Protection should not, however, extend to the point where it eliminates efficiency and competitiveness, or restricts economic expansion. Foreign nationals, who represent a majority of the population, are prohibited from having majority ownership in virtually every business other than certain small service-oriented businesses and may not own property (there are some exceptions for citizens of other GCC states). Kuwait needs to act on proposals such as allowing foreign equity participation in the banking sector (up to 40 percent) and in the upstream oil sector (terms still to be determined).

- Reform the structure of the budget to ensure that most of the nation's revenues and foreign reserves and earnings are integrated into the national budget and into the planning process. Clearly separate royal and national income and investment holdings.

- Place sharp limits on the transfer of state funds to princes and members of the royal family outside the actual ruling family, and transfers of unearned income to members of other leading families. Ensure that such family members are fully taxed on all income and investments.
- Ensure that all income from enterprises with state financing is reflected in the national budget and is integrated into the national economic development and planning program.
- Establish ruthlessly demanding market criteria for evaluating and making all major state and state-supported investments. Require state investments to offer a conclusively higher rate of return than private investments. Demand detailed and independent risk assessment and projections of comparative return on investment, with a substantial penalty for state versus privately funded projects and ventures. Down-size the scale of programs to reduce investment and cash flow costs and the risk of cost-escalation.
- Create new incentives to invest in local industries and business and disincentives for the expatriation of capital.
- Create market driven incentives for foreign investment in major oil and gas projects, refineries, and petrochemical operations. Avoid offset requirements that simply create disguised unemployment or non-competitive ventures that act as a further state-sponsored distortion of the economy.
- Establish a firm rule of law for all property, contract, permitting, and business activity and reduce state bureaucratic and permitting barriers to private investment.
- Place national security spending on the same basis as other state spending, and fully implement the law the National Assembly passed in 1993 to insure that all direct and indirect defense costs— including arms—are reflected in the national budget. Integrate it fully into the national budget, including investment and equipment purchases.
- Replace the present emphasis on judging arms purchases of the basis on initial procurement costs and technical features with a full assessment of life cycle cost—including training, maintenance, and facilities.
- Cease buying arms in an effort to win outside political support and establish with specific procedures and regulations for evaluating the value of standardization and interoperability with existing national equipment and facilities, those of other Gulf states, and those of the US and other power projection forces.

- Subject all offset proposals relating to government military and non-military expenditures abroad to the same risk and cost-benefit analyses used by the private sector, and create independent auditing procedures to ensure that offsets do not become a concealed government subsidy or a way of benefiting influential government officials.
- Expand the number of voters for the National Assembly. Continue to allow the expansion of political activity to ensure the peaceful resolution of internal economic debates.
- Deal with the issue of the Bidoon and expand citizenship to de facto Kuwaitis.
- Create a long-term planning effort focusing on periods five, ten, and twenty years into the future to set goals for Kuwait's social, economic, and military development, with special attention to the problems of population growth, reducing dependence on foreign labor, diversifying the economy, and linking development to a clear set of social goals. Use contingency and risk analysis, not simply growth-oriented models.

At the same time, Kuwait's economic, social, and political reforms must take account of strategic realities. No other country in the Gulf has a clearer need for a strong defense and close security ties to its Southern Gulf neighbors and the West. Kuwait's economic vulnerabilities are not unique, but the same geography that has blessed Kuwait with oil has cursed it with neighbors like Iran and Iraq.[75] Kuwait's oil facilities and urban areas will remain vulnerable to air, missile, armored, and seaborne attack. Kuwait will always be dependent on imports for virtually all of its food. It has no arable land other than a small patch of irrigated land, and only 8% of its territory can be used even for light grazing.

Kuwait's ports will remain within the range of Iranian and Iraqi anti-ship missiles, and Kuwait will have to draw its water from easily targetable desalination plants. Kuwait has only about 0.01 cubic kilometers of internal renewable water resources. This only amounts to about 10 cubic meters per person, one of the lowest levels of any nation in the world.[76] As a result, Kuwait has developed massive desalinization facilities, which have become even more important now that it can no longer import water from Iraq. Kuwait now must import at least 75% of its potable water.[77]

4

Internal Security

Kuwait is taking important steps to broaden its structure of power. The elected National Assembly is increasingly active, and the ruling Al Sabah family is making a slow but steady transition to increased popular participation in government. There is still significant tension, however, between the royal family and some political groups in Kuwait. There is also tension between Kuwait's Sunnis—who control the nation's political leadership and economy—and the Shi'ite portion of the population. These tensions have eased since the liberation, but some problems remain.

Ethnic and Sectarian Divisions

The CIA estimates that about 45% of Kuwait's total population is native Arab, 35% is other Arab, 9% is South Asia, 4% is of Iranian origin, and 7% is "other." Islam is the state religion and the Constitution states that Islamic law, the Shari'a, is "a main source of legislation." The CIA estimates that the Muslim population is about 45% Sunni, 30% Shi'ite, and 10% other Muslim, although the State Department estimates that as many as 40% of Kuwait's population may be Shi'ites.[78] Kuwait has a tiny Arab Christian minority (some of which are native Kuwaitis), which practices freely, and several legally recognized expatriate congregations and churches, including a Catholic diocese, an Anglican church in Ahmadi, and an American-sponsored Protestant church.

The US State Department reports that residents who are members of religions not sanctioned by the Koran (e.g., Hindus, Sikhs, Jews, and Buddhists) may not build places of worship, but may worship in their homes. The Government prohibits missionaries to proselytize among Muslims, but they may serve expatriate congregations. The law prohibits religious education for religions other than Islam, although this law does not appear to be strictly enforced. The Government does not permit the establishment of non-Islamic publishing companies or training institutions for clergy.[79]

The main ethnic division within Kuwait's native population is between Sunni and Shi'ite. The ruling family and many prominent families belong to the denomination of Sunni Islam, and the allocation of government funds favors the Sunni clergy. Shi'ites are free to conduct their liturgies and rites without government interference, and government welfare programs do not discriminate against Shi'ite Muslim citizens. The State Department does report, however, that members of Kuwait's Shi'ite minority are generally underrepresented in high government positions—although two Shi'ite Muslims were appointed to the Cabinet, a Shi'ite has served as oil minister, and a Shi'ite was named to a high-ranking military post in recent years.[80]

Some observers think that the Kuwaiti government has allowed the political police, internal security forces, and royal intelligence to investigate and arrest individual Shi'ites without adequate cause. A number of Kuwaiti Shi'ites have been sentenced for bombing and other terrorist incidents in support of Iran during the Iran-Iraq War, leaving an additional legacy of resentment. These tensions inevitably affect Kuwait's internal security, and may lead to new incidents between Kuwait and Iran over religious issues.

Kuwait also faces major problems in defining its native population. At the end of 1994, there were about 117,000 stateless people in Kuwait, down from the prewar level of about 220,000. Many of these stateless persons are "Bidoon" (the term means "without"). The Bidoon are stateless persons, usually of Iraqi, Jordanian Syrian, or Iranian descent, who resided in Kuwait prior to the Iraqi invasion. The US State Department reports that the Kuwaiti government argues that many of the Bidoon are actually the citizens of other countries, who claim they are stateless in order to remain in Kuwait, become citizens, and enjoy the generous government benefits provided to citizens. Many Bidoon, however, have had residency or ties to Kuwait for generations. Others immigrated to Kuwait during the oil boom years and have effectively been residents for over a decade.[81]

These Bidoon exist in a legal limbo. As long as their citizenship or residency status is undetermined, they do not have a legal right to work or enroll their children in public or private schools. Even Bidoon born of Kuwaiti mothers are denied free education, many job opportunities, social benefits, and sometimes the right to remain in Kuwait unless they are given financial guarantees by a Kuwaiti citizen.[82]

If the Bidoon travel abroad, there is no guarantee that immigration authorities will allow them to reenter Kuwait. Marriage poses special hardships because the offspring of male Bidoon inherit the father's undetermined legal status. The Kuwaiti government has established a review process which would regularize the status of some of the Bidoon and their families, especially for any Bidoon who has served in the military or security forces, and for the children born to marriages between Bidoon men and Kuwaiti women. However, the US State Department reports that this process of regulation is improvised, slow, and ineffective. Kuwaiti government officials claim they recognize the hardships suffered by the Bidoon, but so far have not proposed any remedial legislation.[83]

The Government has eliminated the Bidoon from the census rolls, discontinued their access to government-provided social services, and has sought to deport many Bidoon to other countries. The government also has tried to prevent the return of the Bidoon who departed Kuwait during the Gulf War. It has frequently delayed or denied them entry visas. This policy imposes serious hardships and family separations. In 1993, the government also decreed that Bidoon males may no longer serve in the military services.[84]

The Kuwaiti government has also actively pursued a policy of reducing the number of Iraqis, Palestinians, and other foreign residents since the liberation of Kuwait in 1991. This led to many questionable deportations during 1991–1993 (although many were justified on internal security grounds). Most of the 400,000 pre-war Palestinian and Jordanian workers residing in Kuwait have been forced to leave the country, because of the support that the PLO and Jordan gave to Iraq during the Gulf War. Others have been arrested, and only about 7,000 had work permits in May, 1992.[85]

The Kuwait government now opposes the entry of workers from nations that supported Iraq during the Gulf War, especially Palestinians, Jordanians, and Yemenis. There were still an estimated 36,000 Palestinians in Kuwait in 1996, but the State Department reports that the Kuwaiti government has delayed or denied the issuance of work and residency permits to persons in these groups, and has hindered such workers from sponsoring their families to join them in Kuwait in many cases. The government imposes further hardships by prohibiting schools from enrolling the children of such persons without valid residency permits.

The government did, however, discontinue its postwar practice of arresting and deporting Gazan Palestinians for violating residency laws in 1993. The government issued one year renewable residency permits to 5,000 of the 8,000 Gazans remaining in Kuwait, but did not seek to deport those without residency permits. Even so, a combination of legal and social pressures continues to make many Gazans leave Kuwait.[86]

Dependence on Foreign Labor

Kuwait faces equally serious problems in terms of migration and dependence on a foreign work force, although there is no agreement on the numbers involved. The Kuwaiti Public Authority for Civil Information indicates that 706,994 native Kuwaiti and 1,957,322 expatriate residents lived in Kuwait at the end of 1995. One British estimate indicates that foreigners make up 50–60% of the total population in Kuwait, and that 86% of the work force is foreign.[87] The CIA estimates that Kuwait now has a population of about 1.8 million and a labor force of around 566,000, of which up to 70% may be foreign.[88]

Regardless of any uncertainties over numbers, several things are clear. Kuwait's foreign labor increasingly comes from countries that do not present a threat to Kuwait or a source of potential demands for citizenship.[89] Kuwait's Asian population has increased to about 9% of the total population, with an additional 7% from outside the region.

Kuwait also has taken steps to prevent such workers from becoming a new class of semi-permanent residents and to reduce related state subsidies. Third-country nationals employed in the private sector must earn approximately $2,000 a month, and public sector employees about $1,400 a month, before they can sponsor their families in Kuwait. Resident foreign nationals are subject to stringent visa requirements, special taxes and fees that are intended to both discourage their employment and limit their tenure in Kuwait. Foreign workers also now have to pay for some health services, and Kuwait plans to charge new fees for foreigners in other areas and is considering raising the charges to employers who hire foreign labor.

These measures still, however, leave Kuwait dependent on foreigners for most of its services and industrial labor. This point was illustrated in March, 1995, when approximately 700 KOC workers took part in a weeklong strike to demand pay increases and improved promotional opportunities for Kuwaiti nationals, who hold an estimated 68 percent of the country's oil sector jobs. (Asian expatriates hold the remainder and are paid substantially less.) Although the KOC workers' union claimed that Kuwait's oil production fell by up to 100,000 barrels per day during the strikes, the strikers' jobs were filled temporarily, and no production losses resulted.

However, there are negative side effects from Kuwait's shift to Asian workers. Many of Kuwait's former Palestinian and Jordanian workers regarded themselves as virtual residents, and spent most of their money in Kuwait. In contrast, Asian workers remit most of their earnings home and spend very little in Kuwait. This alters Kuwait's balance of payments and reduces local demand for consumer goods and services.[90]

Kuwait's current level of dependence on foreign labor has resulted in the lack of an effective work ethic among native Kuwaitis, and some estimates indicate that about half of employed Kuwaiti nationals are employed in government or state-owned industries in positions that have no productive output and are little more than disguised unemployment. About 15,500 Kuwait males enter the labor force annually, and, while this number is small and unemployment is currently negligible, Kuwait's current employment structure raises serious questions about its ability to create a productive employment structure for its citizens and offer its youth meaningful career opportunities.

Broadening the Base of Political Power

Under Kuwait's Constitution, the Emir holds executive power and shares legislative power with the National Assembly. The Constitution does, however, give the Emir the power to suspend its provisions and rule by decree. In 1986, the Emir dissolved the National Assembly by suspending the constitutional provisions on the Assembly's election. The Assembly remained dissolved until 1992. The Emir had previously dissolved the Assembly from 1976 to 1981.

In accordance with the practice of the ruling family, the Prime Minister is always the Crown Prince. The Prime Minister currently presides over a 16-member Cabinet, many of whose members come from the Al Sabah family or other leading Sunni families.[91]

Kuwait's political leadership faces increasing demands by its citizens for the sharing of political power. These demands are partly a result of a general desire for political liberalization. However, they reflect criticism by some elements of Kuwait society of the Al Sabah family. Immediately after the liberation, a number of prominent Kuwaiti citizens criticized the royal family for failing to prepare the country for war and for showing inadequate leadership during the fighting. Some elements of the Kuwaiti resistance also felt they were not given proper recognition.

These tensions have resulted in a growing debate over the course of political liberalization that has sometimes involved the US. In June, 1992, the speaker of the National Council criticized the American ambassador for "talking about democracy" and "encouraging the local opposition." Kuwait's first, real post-war election took place in late May 1992. Kuwaiti businessmen voted for the board of the Chamber of Commerce and Industry. This election revealed the extent to which Kuwaiti public opinion called for broader representation. Some 11,500 Kuwaiti businessmen voted, and 23 of 24 seats went to candidates opposed to the current government.

Kuwait held elections for its National Assembly in October, 1992, but these elections were conducted under severe restrictions. The government prohibited political parties, so candidates had to nominate themselves. The Emir blocked plans to organize seminars on the elections and opposition elements were given only limited opportunity to organize.

The voting population was limited to men 21 years or older, who could trace their Kuwaiti residence back to 1920 and had maintained a residence there until 1959. This constituency represented only 81,400 males out of a total population of 600,000, or 13.5% of the population and 30% of adult citizens. Even so, informal political groups were active, 303 candidates ran for the Assembly's 50 seats, and almost the entire franchised male population registered to vote in the election.

The election did little to suppress popular dissent. While the 50 winners of the October 6, 1992, election generally supported continued rule by the royal family, a large majority demanded better government and increased legislative control over the actions of the Emir and senior members of the government. Nine of the 50 new members were Islamists, seven were associated with Islam, 17 had served in the National Assembly which had been suspended by the Emir in 1986, and nine had served in the National Council, a surrogate legislature elected in 1990 by the Emir. This meant that a total of 35 out of 50 members were Islamists, traditional politicians, and secular liberals who had previously called for a parliament that could put stronger checks and balances on the government.[92]

Since 1992, the Kuwaiti parliament has steadily increased its power. It has held heated debates over the issue of power sharing, the fiscal accountability of the Al Sabah family, and whether an open investigation should be held into the events leading to Kuwait's state of unpreparedness on August 2, 1990. The Assembly has begun to participate in major budget and resource decisions, and has actively debated corruption and waste in defense spending, the sharing of the nation's wealth, the royal family's management of the Fund for the Future Generations and Kuwait's national investments, the repayment of debts owed because of the collapse of Kuwait's stock market, the way in which privatization is conducted, and the amount of money that should be spent on military forces. It has reshaped the repayment deadlines on Kuwait's "difficult debt" and the outcome of many other important issues.[93]

The National Assembly has also broadened the base of the Kuwaiti electorate. In 1994 the Assembly passed legislation extending the right to vote to the sons of naturalized Kuwaiti citizens—about 110,000 males. According to the 1994 law, citizens who have been naturalized citizens for at least 30 years will also be eligible to vote in 1996.[94] A majority of candidates elected in 1992 have also stated that they favor extending the vote to women, although proposals to do so have been delayed in a legislative committee. The Emir and the Prime Minister have publicly stated that they support political rights for women, but have made no apparent effort to persuade the National Assembly.[95]

Kuwait is slowly developing the equivalent of political parties. The government officially bans political parties, but several informal blocs have arisen that act like parties. These blocs played a major role in the 1992 elections and in the succeeding National Assembly sessions. The government has made no effort to limit these groupings, which are organized on the basis of common ideological goals. Many play a role as "opposition" groups.

Public gatherings still must receive prior government approval, as must private gatherings of more than five persons that result in the issuance of a public statement. As a result, most popular political activity takes the form of family-based, almost exclusively male, social gatherings known as "diwaniyas." Most male adults, including the Emir, host and attend diwaniyas, which discuss every possible topic. Since 1994, these diwanyas have increasingly been focused on the 1996 election and have been more critical of the current members of National Assembly. There is growing public debate over the failure of the Assembly to take decisive action on the budget deficit, halt waste and graft, the future of the Bidoon, and the use of the assets of the Kuwaiti Investment Authority.[96]

These trends towards increased power sharing seem likely to help Kuwait cope with the socio-economic changes it must make over the coming decades, rather than to threaten the regime or Kuwait's political stability. Kuwait has the freest political climate of any Southern Gulf country, and permits far more freedom of media and academic debate than its neighbors. It is also clear that the campaign for its October 5, 1996, National Assembly elections are certain to be vigorous—to say the least.

At the same time, there are reports that members of the royal family oppose the current level of freedom for the National Assembly, and some have called for its suppression. Kuwait also still has some human rights problems. The Kuwaiti government dissolved a number of unlicensed political groups in August, 1993—including the Kuwaiti Association to Defend War Victims, a major human rights group. This led to the resignation of the members of the Hostages and Missing Committee of the National Assembly. Organizations like Amnesty International also claim that the government has hundreds of political prisoners, and that the State Security Court that tried Iraqi collaborators and other persons charged with national security crimes, abuses human rights.[97]

5

Kuwait's Military Forces

Kuwait faces potential threats from Iran and Iraq that make it the most vulnerable country in the Gulf. Table Eight shows the size of Kuwait's forces relative to potential threats from Iran and Iraq. This table makes it clear that Kuwait must do everything it can to strengthen its forces if it is to develop its collective security capabilities, maintain its sovereignty, reinforce its deterrence of Iran and Iraq, and deal with low-level threats and incursions.

At the same time, Table Eight shows that there is no foreseeable point at which Kuwait, or any combination of Kuwait and the other Southern Gulf states, can provide Kuwait with security against Iraq or secure Kuwait's access through the Gulf. Kuwait is one of the most strategically exposed states in the world, and nothing it can do by itself will give it the ability to defend against Iran and Iraq. Its vulnerability is one of the central realities affecting any effort to create a stable mix of deterrent and defensive capabilities in the Gulf.

Iraq's invasion provided a brutal demonstration of that vulnerability. Kuwait, the other Southern Gulf states, and the West must clearly recognize this strategic imperative if any effort to encourage regional stability is to succeed. Kuwait was unprepared for the invasion despite the fact that several Kuwait commanders had advised Kuwait to put its forces on the alert and move them into defensive positions. As a result, the bulk of Kuwait's military forces disintegrated during the first hours of Iraq's invasion. Much of Kuwait's military equipment was captured and much of the rest was lost or destroyed. Only some of its aircraft, a few vessels, and a limited amount of land equipment escaped to Saudi Arabia.

Since the Gulf War, Kuwait has attempted to rebuild its forces and correct many of the military weaknesses that existed at the time of the Iraqi invasion. In August 1995, Kuwait's Minister of Defense, Sheik Ahmad Hamoud al-Jaber al-Sabah announced that Kuwait's army had recovered 85% of the effectiveness it had had before the Iraqi invasion, that Kuwait hoped to fully rebuild its forces over the next few years, and that, "the

TABLE EIGHT Gulf Military Forces in 1996

	Iran	Iraq	Bahrain	Kuwait	Oman	Qatar	Saudi Arabia*	UAE	Yemen
Manpower									
Total Active	513,000	382,500	10,700	16,600	43,500	11,100	161,500	70,000	39,500
Regular	393,000	382,500	10,700	16,600	37,000	11,100	105,500	70,000	39,500
National Guard & Other	120,000	0	0	0	6,500	0	57,000	0	0
Reserve	350,000	650,000	0	23,700	0	0	0	0	40,000
Paramilitary	200,000	24,800	9,250	5,200	4,400	0	15,500	2,700	30,000
Army and Guard									
Manpower	446,000	350,000	8,500	10,000	31,500	8,500	127,000	65,000	37,000
Regular Army Manpower	345,000	350,000	8,500	10,000	25,000	8,500	70,000	65,000	37,000
Reserve	350,000	450,000	0	0	0	0	20,000	0	40,000
Tanks	1,445	2,700	106	220	91	24	910	133	1,125
AIFV/Recce, Lt. Tanks	515	2,400	46	130	55	50	1,467	515	580
APCs	550	2,000	235	199	53	172	3,670	380	560
Self Propelled Artillery	289	230	13	38	6	28	200	90	30
Towed Artillery	1,995	1,500	36	0	96	12	270	82	483
MRLs	664	250	9	0	0	4	60	48	220
Mortars	3,500	2,700	18	24	74	39	400	101	800
SSM Launchers	46	12	0	0	0	0	10	6	30
Light SAM Launchers	700	800	65	48	62	58	650	36	700
AA Guns	1,700	5,500	0	0	18	12	10	62	372
Air Force Manpower	18,000	15,000	1,500	2,500	4,100	800	18,000	3,500	1,000
Air Defense Manpower	12,000	15,000	0	0	0	0	4,000	0	0

(continues)

TABLE EIGHT *(continued)*

	Iran	Iraq	Bahrain	Kuwait	Oman	Qatar	Saudi Arabia*	UAE	Yemen
Total Combat Aircraft	295	353	24	76	46	12	295	97	69
Bombers	0	6	0	0	0	0	0	0	0
Fighter/Attack	150	130	12	40	19	11	112	41	27
Fighter/Interceptor	115	180	12	8	0	1	122	22	30
Recce/FGA Recce	8	0	0	0	12	0	10	8	0
AEW/C4I/BM	1	0	0	0	0	5	0	0	0
MR/MPA**	6	0	0	0	7	0	0	0	0
OCU/COIN	0	18	0	11	13	0	36	15	0
Combat Trainers	92	75	0	11	22	0	66	35	12
Transport Aircraft**	68	34	3	4	14	5	49	20	19
Tanker Aircraft	4	2	0	0	0	0	16	0	0
Armed Helicoptors**	100	120	10	16	0	20	12	42	8
Other Helicopters**	509	350	8	36	37	7	138	42	21
Major SAM Launchers	204	260	12	24	0	0	128	18	87
Light SAM Launchers	60	60	0	12	28	9	249	34	0
AA Guns	0	0	0	12	0	0	420	0	0
Navy Manpower	38,000	2,500	700	1,500	4,200	1,800	13,500	1,500	1,500
Major Surface Combatants									
Missile	5	0	3	0	0	0	8	3	0
Other	2	1	0	0	0	0	0	0	0
Patrol Craft									
Missile	10	1	4	2	4	3	9	8	7

(continues)

TABLE EIGHT (continued)

	Iran	Iraq	Bahrain	Kuwait	Oman	Qatar	Saudi Arabia[*]	UAE	Yemen
Other	26	7	4	12	8	6	20	9	3
Submarines	2	0	0	0	0	0	0	0	0
Mine Vessels	3	4	0	0	0	0	7	0	3
Amphibious Vessels	8	0	0	0	2	0	0	0	2
Landing Craft	17	3	4	6	4	1	8	4	2

Notes: Does not include equipment in storage. Air Force totals include all helicopters, and all heavy surface-to-air missile launchers.

[*]60,000 reserves are National Guard Tribal Levies. The total for land forces includes active National Guard equipment. These additions total 262 AIFVs, 1,165 APCs, and 70 towed artillery weapons.

[**]Includes navy, army, national guard, and royal flights, but not paramilitary.

Source: Adapted by Anthony H. Cordesman from International Institute for Strategic Studies *Military Balance* (IISS, London), in this case, the 1995–1996 edition; *Military Technology, World Defense Almanac, 1994–1995*; and Jaffee Center for Strategic Studies, *The Military Balance in the Middle East, 1993–1994* (JCSS, Tel Aviv, 1994).

Kuwait army is capable of safeguarding the security of Kuwait's borders and appropriately responding to any enemy movements, supported by brothers in the GCC and friendly troops in the region."[98]

Kuwait's military forces have been rebuilt and improved to the point where they can play animportant role in demonstrating that Kuwait has the will to protect its sovereignty. They are developing an improved ability to deal with the kind of threatening movements, infiltrations, and low-level attacks that Iran and Iraq can use to intimidate Kuwait.

Kuwait's forces will, however, always be too weak to defend so vulnerable a geographic position. Kuwait is also having to reformulate the over-ambitious and unrealistic plans for a 40,000 men force structure and major equipment purchases it developed after the Gulf War. As a result, Kuwait faces hard trade-offs between domestic and external politics, the structural limits on its force expansion capabilities, and its security needs.

Kuwait's Borders

Kuwait cannot overcome the basic strategic reality that it is a small country with immense wealth with the wrong neighbors. Kuwait's total territory is only about 17,800 square kilometers, or roughly the size of New Jersey, but Kuwait has a 240 kilometer long border with Iraq and a 222 kilometer border with Saudi Arabia. These borders present major problems for Kuwait in preventing infiltrations and raids.

Since the Gulf War, Kuwait has attempted to improve the security of its border by creating a 207–218 kilometer long ditch, sand wall, and barbed wire fence to demarcate its border with Iraq. In mid-1995, it had nearly completed construction of a system with a three meter deep trench, followed by a five meter sand berm, equipped with sensors to detect the movement of vehicles.[99] Kuwait also built a patrol road along the border with observation posts and monitoring sensors. This security system is operated by the Ministry of Interior, and is similar to one under consideration by Saudi Arabia.

It is not clear exactly what sensors Kuwait is now using or plans to buy in the future. If the security zone is equipped with all of the technology that was discussed during plans for its construction, it will have IR sensors, pressure sensors, electrified wires, trenches, barbed wire and electronic sensors. Contending companies proposed different approaches to creating such a system. Thomson-CSF and Thorn favored infra-red sensors. Racal Comsec and Hughes favored terrestrial and pressure cable sensors, and some experts preferred tethered aerostats carrying radars.

Kuwait is also studying options for the creation of a second defense barrier designed to slow an armored advance and equipped with mines and other anti-armor barriers. According to some reports, work has begun on such defenses.

Kuwait reports that its security system has been valuable in reducing border infiltrations. These have dropped from several hundred a year during 1992–1994 to a few incidents a week in the spring of 1995. This drop, however, may also be the result of Iraqi efforts to persuade the UN to ease its sanctions and the improved efforts of UN forces to secure the border area.[100]

In any case, Kuwait's borders will still be highly vulnerable to rapid armored attacks. Kuwait's terrain consists largely of slightly undulating desert plains, and has few defensive barriers. The only significant elevation in the country is the Al-Mutla Ridge, just north of the city of Al Jahra. The pass through this ridge from the north into Kuwait City is the only real defensive position against Iraq. The gorge of Al Batin (Hafr al-Batin) forms only a limited barrier to the west. The one defensive line north of the Bay of Kuwait provides only a limited advantage to the defender, and the road net between Kuwait City and Basra in Iraq allows rapid movement of troops.

The desert in Northern Kuwait permits relatively easy movement by armor, and there are a number of highways and major road links in the area. Kuwait has some 3,000 kilometers of roads, 2,500 kilometers of which are paved. There are far fewer routes going into Kuwait from the West, but the British army demonstrated during the Gulf War that a modern armored force can cross the Hafr al Batin gorge relatively easily, and US forces showed that an armored force can move relatively rapidly from positions in Iraq to the Saudi border by passing Kuwait to the west.

Kuwait's Forces and Strategic Vulnerabilities

This geography not only demands strong forces, but forces with high readiness and rapid deployment capability. Kuwait's land forces can only be effective if they are able to deploy to their defensive positions before Iraq attacks. Kuwait's air and naval forces must also be capable of moving to full combat readiness in a matter of hours. Kuwaiti air space is very vulnerable, and Kuwait is vulnerable to heliborne and air assault. It has seven airfields, four of which are paved and have runways 2,400–3,439 meters long. There are many areas in Kuwait where paved roads and areas allow rapid movement by helicopter. Most of Kuwait's territorial waters and port areas are vulnerable to long-range anti-ship missiles launched from nearby positions in Iran and Iraq. Kuwait has relatively good maritime surveillance capabilities, but its navigation channels are vulnerable to covert minelaying by small craft, and much of its 499 kilometer coastline has areas where amphibious craft or raiding parties can land.

Kuwait's dependence on electric power and desalination plants increases its vulnerability, and its refineries and oil port are potential hostages to air and missile attacks from Iran and Iraq. Ships moving into Kuwait's three oil ports at Mina Abdullah, (Seal Island), Mina Saud, and Mina al Ahmadi (North Pier) can also be attacked by long-range anti-ship missiles. Kuwait also faces problems in defending Bubiyan and Warbah—its two large main islands in the salt marshes north of Kuwait. These are low lying sand islands with large amounts of salt marsh. They have no economic value, but they control the channel to Umm Qasr, Iraq's only naval base with direct access to the Gulf. Both Iran and Iraq have posed potential threats to these islands in the past.

6

Kuwaiti Military Spending and Arms Imports

These threats and the shock of Iraq's invasion explain the trends in Kuwaiti military spending and arms imports. Kuwait has been forced to shift from a strategy of accommodating its more powerful neighbors to one of strengthening its own forces and paying part of the cost of US presence and power projection. The result has sharply increased the amount Kuwait must spend on military preparedness.

Military Spending

A US estimate of Kuwaiti central government spending, military spending, deliveries of military imports, and total export earnings is shown in Chart Thirteen. These trends are shown in constant 1993 dollars, and reflect the fact that Kuwaiti military expenditures took up only a relatively moderate share of Kuwaiti central government expenditures and arms imports until the Gulf War.

Chart Fourteen shows the trends in per capita GDP and military expenditure per capita in constant dollars and provides a similar picture of the burden military spending has placed on Kuwait in recent years. As has been discussed earlier, the Gulf War placed a catastrophic burden on the Kuwaiti economy and budget, although Kuwaiti exports recovered relatively quickly and military spending dropped sharply after 1993.

According to US estimates, Kuwait spent over $1 billion annually on military forces (in current dollars) beginning in the early 1980s. It spent around $1.5 billion during 1983–1985—the period when it felt most threatened by Iran. ACDA estimates that Kuwait spent $766 million on defense in 1979, $892 million in 1980. $886 million in 1981, $1,157 million in 1982, $1,446 million in 1983, $1,415 million in 1984, $1,509 million in 1985, $1,287 million in 1986, $1,250 million in 1987, $1,1260 million in 1988, and $1,944 million in 1989. These expenditures averaged around

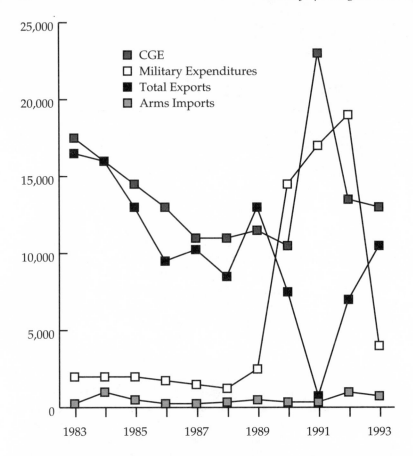

CHART THIRTEEN   Kuwaiti Military Expenditures, Total Imports, and Arms
Imports: 1983–1993 (Constant $93 Millions). *Source:* Adapted by Anthony H.
Cordesman from ACDA, *World Military Expenditures and Arms Transfers,
1993–1994,* ACDA/GPO, Washington, 1995.

5%–6% of Kuwait's GDP, and 12% to 14% of its central government
expenditures.[101]

These military expenditures rose to dramatic new heights after Iraq's
invasion of Kuwait. ACDA estimates that Kuwait spent $13,240 million in
1990 and $16,030 million in 1991 to reequip and retrain its forces, and to
provide aid to other Coalition forces. It spent $19,090 billion in 1992,
largely on new orders of equipment to support its post–Gulf War modernization plans. Spending then dropped back to $3.604 billion in 1993,
and $3.086 billion in 1994.

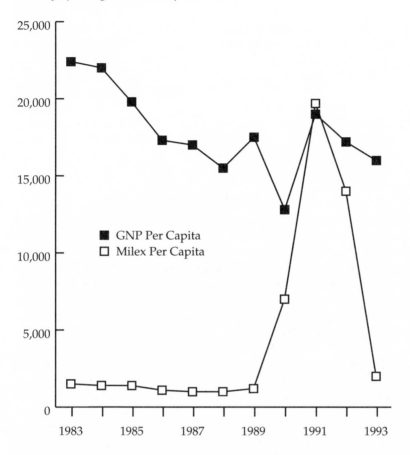

CHART FOURTEEN Kuwaiti GNP Per Capita Versus Military Expenditures Per Capita (Constant $93). *Source:* Adapted by Anthony H. Cordesman from ACDA, *World Military Expenditures and Arms Transfers, 1993–1994,* Washington, ACDA-GPO, 1995, Table I.

According to Kuwaiti figures, military spending dropped back towards prewar levels in 1993, with expenditures of $1.8 billion. They dropped to a base level of $1.7 billion in 1994, and were estimated to be $1.65 billion in 1995. These figures, however, exclude some capital costs for arms expenditures, many construction and infrastructure costs, and a wide range of related service costs. The IISS estimates that Kuwait spent $3.01 billion in 1993, $3.09 billion in 1994, and $2.91 billion in 1995. Some US experts believe that Kuwait's total military spending had continued to total over $5 billion a year since 1993.[102]

Total Kuwaiti military spending reached $5.4 billion in 1994–1995—including a $778 million emergency increase to cover the unexpected cost of the Kuwaiti deployment to counter Iraq's October, 1994 build-up on Kuwait's border. It is not clear whether some $500 million in additional spending to pay for the deployment of US and other allied forces is included in this total or has simply been taken from Kuwait's General Reserve. Even these figures, however, mean that Kuwait is spending about $1,907 per capita on military forces, versus $1,335 for Israel and $1,204 for the US.[103]

Kuwait Arms Expenditures

Kuwait's effort to reequip and expand its forces have also been costly and have led to a bitter debate between the government and the National Assembly over how much Kuwait should spend on arms.[104] In 1992, the Emir issued a decree that called for Kuwait to spend roughly $11.8 billion on arms over the next twelve years. This plan met with strong objections from the National Assembly once it came to office. The Assembly criticized both the total amount and the way in which the government selected weapons and military contractors.

The Finance and Economy Committee of the National Assembly rejected the Ministry of Defense's proposal to spend the money allowed under the decree in July, 1993, and raised a wide range of issues about the government's plans and methods of allocating contracts. As a result, funding of the modernization plan was delayed until April, 1994, when the National Assembly voted an $11.7 billion supplementary defense budget to be spent in increments over a 10 year period, and with enhanced supervision by the National Assembly. This compromise came only after the government agreed to notify the National Assembly of each year's spending from the supplementary budget and the defense minister, Ali Salem al-Sabah, was forced to switch places with the interior minister, Ahmad Hamoud al-Jaber al-Sabah, because of Salem's resistance to any compromise with the National Assembly.[105]

The compromise raises questions about Kuwait's future ability to fund its force expansion plans. By the time the National Assembly approved the compromise, Kuwait had already spent billions of dollars on new arms, and the $11.7 billion approved by the National Assembly also has to cover the cost of exercises with the US, and US prepositioning in Kuwait—which includes a $300 million prepositioning facility for a US mechanized brigade to be located south of Kuwait City.[106] While the numbers are suspect, Kuwait has reported that it spent $396 million on procurement outlays for arms in FY1994–

FY1995, and may spend only $330 million in FY1995–FY1996.[107] As a result, the total funds available may not meet Kuwait's needs for new equipment.

It is difficult to separate Kuwait's expenditures on arms from its purchases of military equipment for allied countries during the period of the Gulf War, but an ACDA estimate of the value of arms deliveries to Kuwait in constant 1993 dollars is shown in Chart Thirteen. ACDA also estimates that Kuwait took delivery on $60 million worth of arms in current dollars in 1979, $40 million in 1980, $120 million in 1981, $110 million in 1982, $130 million in 1983, $650 million in 1984, $370 million in 1985, $180 million in 1986, $200 million in 1987, $260 million in 1988, $470 million in 1989, $280 million in 1990, $480 million in 1991, $1,000 million in 1992, $750 million in 1993, and $250 million in 1994. These data on deliveries do not reflect the full outyear cost of major Kuwaiti orders during the late 1980s, or the surge in Kuwaiti orders after the Gulf War, because of the delay between orders and deliveries and because Kuwait has structured its payment schedules to avoid massive orders in a single year.[108]

ACDA indicates that Kuwait has shifted the source of its arms imports as a result of the Gulf War. Kuwait took delivery on $1,345 million worth of arms (in current dollars) during 1985–1989—the period before the Gulf War. Only $150 million worth came from the US, with $180 million worth coming from Russia, $450 million coming from France, $110 million coming from the UK, $5 million from Eastern Europe, $20 million from other European countries, and $430 million from other Middle Eastern countries like Egypt.[109]

In contrast, most of Kuwait's deliveries since the Gulf War have come from the US. ACDA indicates that Kuwait took delivery on $2,040 million worth of arms transfers between 1992–1994. A total of $1,800 million came from the US, $100 million from France, and $140 million from other states.[110] Kuwait's arms deliveries during 1992–1994 had a similar pattern. They had a total worth of $2.040 billion. Kuwait received $1.8 billion worth of arms from the US, $100 million from France, $30 million from other Middle Eastern countries, $80 million from East European countires, and $30 million from other states.[111]

Recent reporting by Richard F. Grimmett of the Congressional Research Service is summarized in Chart Fifteen. This chart indicates that Kuwait signed a total of $5.7 billion worth of new arms agreements during 1991–1994, versus a total of $3.8 billion during 1987–1990—a similar period before the Gulf War. Kuwait placed nearly $3.4 billion of these orders in 1993 alone. As a result, Kuwait ranked third in world arms agreements during 1990–1993, although it did not number among the top ten nations in 1986–1989.[112]

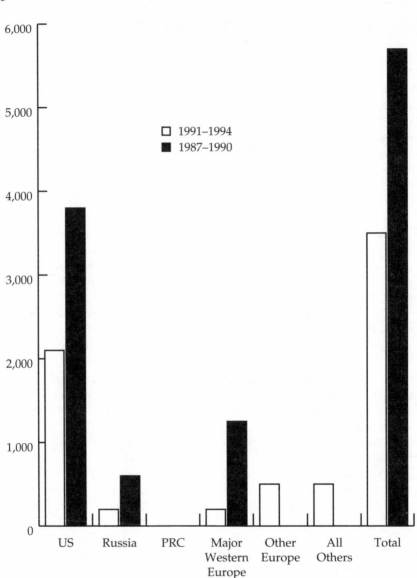

CHART FIFTEEN Kuwaiti Arms Sales Agreements by Supplier Country: 1987–1994 ($Current Millions). *Source:* Adapted by Anthony H. Cordesman from work by Richard F. Grimmett in *Conventional Arms Transfers to Developing Nations, 1987–1994,* Congressional Research Service 95-862F, August 4, 1994, pp. 56–57.

Kuwait's Recent Major Arms Purchases

Table Nine provides a list of Kuwait's recent major arms purchases. This list shows that Kuwait's purchases are more focused on its military needs than those of many Gulf countries, but it reflects the problems that are typical of all Southern Gulf states. Kuwait buys from too many countries and buys too many specialized items of military equipment that are not fully standardized and interoperable within its own forces.

The lack of substantive progress in coordinating and standardizing the forces of the Gulf Cooperation Council means that there is no overall standardization of Kuwait's forces and those of other Gulf states—although there is limited standardization with the forces of Saudi Arabia—the only state with land and air forces large and effective enough to make a major difference in the event of a large-scale Iraqi or Iranian attack. Similarly, the lack of overall progress in the coordination of Gulf forces means that Kuwait's purchases are not part of any major mission system, whether air defense, mine warfare, maritime surveillance or air attack. This lack of true systems integration and standardization forces Kuwait into major diseconomies of scale, as it does all of the Southern Gulf states.

As might be expected, there is also only partial standardization with US land and air forces, which now seem likely to be the only major Western power projection forces that will support Kuwait in a major contingency. Further, the items listed provide strong signs that Kuwait is returning to the pattern of making political purchases from every important trading partner and supplier state—a pattern that may be good politics but further complicates Kuwait's problems with sustainability and interoperability.

Table Nine shows that the impact of the National Assembly has not been particularly productive in improving the quality of Kuwait's arms purchases. Kuwait's down-sizing of its military modernization increasingly seems to be more political than functional. Spending limits are only being applied with limited regard to Kuwait's military needs, and the resulting problems are being compounded by a growing tendency to buy from certain countries to try to obtain their diplomatic support.

Further, Kuwait is coming under increasing pressure from European, Chinese, and other sellers to buy for such reasons. For example, French President Jacques Chirac intervened in a competition between France's Aerospatiale and British Aerospace Dynamics in February, 1996. The competition was over the sale of the MM-15 versus the Sea Skua missile, and Chirac argued that Kuwait had agreed to give all naval contracts to France for a period of 10 years. This is precisely the kind of arms sale policies that *no* Gulf state should pursue, and it may ultimately cost Kuwait far more in lives than it saves in Dinars.[113]

TABLE NINE   Key Kuwaiti Equipment Developments

- 218 M-1A2 US-made Abrams tanks.
- Kuwait has given up plans to replace its low quality Yugoslav M-84 supplied tanks with 100–150 more M-1A2s.
- Purchasing 254 British Warrior AIFVs ($918 million), but it has given up plans to standardize on the Warrior, and buy the 450–600 it once considered.
- Filling out its armored strength by buying 125 M-113 APCs, 40 BMP-2, and 20 BMP-3s.
- Plans to procure up to 263 wheeled armored vehicles.
- Taking delivery on large numbers of TOW and HOT, and at least 200 Carl Gustav 84 mm rocket launchers. Evaluating purchase of the Milan 3.
- Has reduced plans for major order of new self-propelled-artillery weapons, but is considering purchase of 24 more 155 mm artillery systems. It is studying the purchase of US, South African, and Swiss systems. It is also studying upgrading its M-109 155 mm self-propelled howitzers to the M-109A6 Paladin improvement package or to use the VSEL AS90 155 mm turret. Kuwait is also attempting to sell its Auf-1s and replace them with the Giat Caesar 52 155 mm self-propelled or 155 TR towed weapon, and is considering a GIAT offer to modernize its AuF-3s.
- Ordered MLRS in 1989, but had to cancel the order because of cost. It has ordered 27 Russian BM 30 9A52-2 Smerch multiple rocket launchers to equip three multiple launcher batteries in a separate regiment, but Kuwait may not implement the order. Reported to be considering the purchase of the Russian SS-200 ground-to-ground missile, and/or Sakr-36 and Fatih rocket launchers from Egypt. Considering the purchase of a UAV for artillery targeting and surveillance purposes.
- Ordered 48 Shorts Starburst manportable anti-aircraft missile fire units and 300 missiles and considering additional purchases of Starburst or Mistral Atlas. Also considering the purchase of four batteries of ADATS, Roland-3 with VT-1 missiles, Alenia Aramais, or AdSAMS—which fires the Aim-120 AMRAAM.
- 8 Combattante-I 225-ton missile patrol boats.
- 5 South Korean Seagull class patrol boats.
- Studying orders of 4–6 88–95 meter offshore missile vessels displacing 1,500 to 2,000 tons.
- Other purchase plans include amphibious landing ships, naval helicopters with anti-ship missiles, and a wide range of new weapons systems and sensors.
- 32 US F/A-18C and 8 F/A-18D fighters, AIM-9 Sidewinder air-to-air missiles, AIM-7F Sparrows, AGM-84 Harpoon anti-ship missiles, and Maverick AGM-65G anti-ship/anti-hard point missiles.
- Discussing longer term plans to order up to 35 more fighters, and may make an initial buy of 12 F/A-18C/D aircraft. Seeking to buy the AMRAAM and considering a possible buy of the Mirage 2000-5 multi-role fighter. Seeking to fund such purchases by selling its remaining Skyhawks and Mirage F-1CTKs.

(continues)

TABLE NINE   (*continued*)

- Studying possible purchase of airborne alert aircraft and/or maritime patrol aircraft. It may purchase the E-2C.
- Would like to buy Hawk 100 trainers, or at least upgrade its Mark 64s.
- Considering the purchase of six more transports—probably C-130s and/or Shorts Sherpas.
- Originally examined the purchase of 16–20 AH-64A Apache attack helicopters. Decided on 16 Blackhawk UH-60L helicopters with 500 Hellfire anti-armor missiles, 38 Hellfire launchers, 11,500 Hydra rockets, 200 mm gun pods, and night vision devices. Considering a follow-on purchase of the AH-64A or additional UH-60Ls in the mid-term. It is also considering the purchase of AS-532 Cougar, Black Hawk, and IAR IAR-530 transport helicoptors.
- Kuwait signed a contract with Hughes in December, 1992 to create a new land-based early warning system, refurbish an air operations center, and construct a new radar site. The first phase of the new system—the Radar Preliminary Early Warning System (RPEWS)—became operational in 1994. The system is shelter mounted, and integrates two of Kuwait's main search radars: A new AN/FPS-117 L-Band radar with a radome antenna and an existing French TSR-2100 Tiger S-Band radar at Kuwait City. Work is also underway to integrate an airborne L-88 L-Band radar, mounted in an aerostat, into the system. Kuwait ordered a long-range Thomson-CSF TRS 22XX S-Band radar.
- 5 batteries of Patriot surface-to-air missiles, with 210 MIM-104 PAC-2 GEMs (Guidance Enhancement Missiles). Kuwait has considered buying six new batteries of I-Hawk Phase III fire units and 342 MIM-23B Hawk missiles as well, but delayed this decision pending a study of possible reconstruction of the equipment for four I-Hawk batteries which Iraq returned after the war. According to some reports, it is considering an order for Russian SA-10 or SA-12 (S-300PU) missiles.

Kuwait's Arms Purchases from the US

Kuwait's imports from the US rose from $2.2 billion in 1986–1989 to $3.8 billion in 1990–1993, and did not rank among the top 10 in signing new arms agreements in 1994. Grimmett's data, which are rounded to the nearest $100 million, indicate Kuwait bought $3.9 billion of the $5.7 billion total from the US, $600 million from Russia, and $1,200 million from major West European nations, including Britain, France, Germany, and Italy.[114]

Kuwait's arms deliveries during 1991–1994 had a total worth of $2.5 billion—reflecting the lag between new orders and deliveries. It received $2.1 billion worth of arms from the US, $200 million from major Western European countries, $100 million from other European countries, and $100 million from other states.[115]

The recent trends in Kuwaiti military imports from the US are summarized in Table Ten. Reporting by the US Defense Security Assistance Agency reflects the fact that Kuwait signed major orders for US F/A-18 aircraft before the Gulf War, and major new FMS sales agreements following its liberation after the Gulf War. Kuwait ordered $2.9 billion worth of arms in fiscal year 1993, although orders dropped to more normal levels in FY1994.

The rate of US deliveries to Kuwait, shows far less of a rise because of the slow delivery of the F/A-18, and the fact that the main surge in Kuwaiti orders following the Gulf War did not take place until FY1993. All US sales to Kuwait are cash transactions. Kuwait does not make use of the International Military Education and Training (IMET) program, and has received no recent Military Assistance Program (MAP) aid.[116]

TABLE TEN US Foreign Military Sales (FMS), Commercial Arms Export Agreements, Military Assistance Programs (MAP), and International Military Education and Training (IMET) Programs with Kuwait: FY1985–1994 ($Current Millions)

	1985	1986	1987	1988	1989	1990	1991	1992	1993	1994
Foreign Military Financing Program Payment Waived										
DoD Direct	—	—	—	—	—	—	—	—	—	—
DoD Guarantee	—	—	—	—	—	—	—	—	—	—
FMS Agreements	99.9	140.5	56.6	1,915.4	91.0	55.2	156.8	470.5	2,871.6	182.8
Commercial Sales	3.9	8.8	3.9	2.9	1.5	3.5	2.3	7.4	1.7	0.1
FMS Construction Agreements	—	—	—	4.2	—	—	123.4	15.8	6.5	—
FMS Deliveries	33.7	67.3	58.4	41.0	46.4	51.5	75.9	815.0	829.6	225.5
MAP Program	—	—	—	—	—	—	—	—	—	—
MAP Deliveries	—	—	—	—	—	—	—	—	—	—
MAP Excess Defense Articles Program	—	—	—	—	—	—	—	—	—	—
MAP Excess Defense Articles Deliveries	—	—	—	—	—	—	—	—	—	—
IMET Program/ Deliveries	—	—	—	—	—	—	—	—	—	—

Source: Adapted from US Defense Security Assistance Agency (DSAA), "Foreign Military Sales, Foreign Military Construction Sales, and Military Assistance Facts as of September 30, 1994," Department of Defense, Washington, 1995.

7

Kuwait's Military Forces
Before the Gulf War

Kuwait faces unique challenges in utilizing these arms orders and rebuilding its military forces. The Gulf War destroyed much of Kuwait's military capability in August, 1990, and has forced Kuwait to try to recreate many of its previous military capabilities while it is simultaneously being forced to add new forces and capabilities to deal with the threat from Iran and Iraq. Some of the problems Kuwait has encountered in meeting these challenges are the inevitable result of a small nation trying to deal with major threats in the midst of post-war reconstruction. Other problems Kuwait encountered long before the Gulf War. Thus it is necessary to understand the pre-war strengths and weaknesses of Kuwait's forces in order to understand current military developments in Kuwait.

Kuwait's military forces had a paper strength of around 20,000 men at the time Iraq invaded. This manpower included large numbers of Bedouins who were not full citizens. Kuwait was heavily dependent on foreign personnel for its technical support, service and logistic support, maintenance, and training. These support personnel included Jordanians, Pakistanis, and Egyptians, some of whom were of mediocre quality. There were US, British, and French military and contractor missions for virtually all of Kuwait's more advanced and Western-supplied military equipment. However, these teams only provided technical support and often experienced problems with Kuwait's bureaucracy.

Kuwait did have a number of well trained officers, some of whom attended Sandhurst. Other Officers, and some NCOs and technicians, had trained in the US, Pakistan, and Jordan. The officer corps and NCOs were relatively loyal and were recruited from the ruling family and loyal tribes. Unfortunately, recruitment and promotion were often dominated by favoritism, rather than performance. Kuwait also had severe difficulty recruiting its citizens into the military. Its population before the Iraqi invasion was only about 2.2 million, and less than 30% of this was native

Kuwaiti. Only about 19,500 males reached military age in 1990, and the total male work force from ages 15 to 49—including expatriates—totaled only about 442,000.[117]

While Kuwait tried to get its citizens to join the armed forces by offering good pay and privileges, few volunteered in a country that offered so many more rewarding alternatives. In theory, Kuwait had a draft requiring two years of service, except for university students—who only had to serve one year. There were so many exemptions, however, that the draft existed largely on paper. As a result, most of the "Kuwaitis" in the military forces in 1990 were from tribal groups that were not really citizens. These Bedouin were raised as tribal levies and had no reason to be loyal to the Kuwaiti government. They were poorly treated and paid, and often deserted.

The Kuwaiti Army Before the Gulf War

When the Gulf War began, Kuwait's total army manpower was less than 16,000 men. While Kuwait's order of battle had two armored brigades, one mechanized brigade, and an artillery brigade with a self-propelled artillery regiment and one surface-to-surface missile battalion, the reality was little more than a hollow shell. Its total army manpower was equivalent to only two Western brigades, and all of its units were seriously undermanned.

Kuwait had limited ability to employ its strength of 275 main battle tanks (of which 165 were first-line Chieftains, 70 were low quality Vickers Mark 1s, and 40 were obsolete Centurions), effectively in anything other than a set-piece defense. Even its Chieftain tanks were underpowered and experienced continuous overheating and maintenance problems.[118] Kuwait had ordered the Yugoslav M-84, a variant of the early Soviet T-72, as a replacement tank, but these were not in service. The M-84 has a fire control system superior to any T-72s found in Iraq's arsenal and has a much more powerful engine. With the addition of better ammunition, the M-84 would prove to be far more capable than many T-72s.

Kuwait had more capability to use its lighter armor, but only in set-piece defensive maneuvers. This armor included 50 BMP-2 and 100 AT-105 Saxon and Saladin armored fighting vehicles, 100 Saracen and 200 M-113 APCs, and 90 Ferret armored cars. It had British Scorpions and Soviet BMP-2 armored fighting vehicles on order.[119] Kuwait had bought a wide range of anti-tank weapons, including the AT-4, BGM-71A Improved TOW, HOT, M-47 Dragon, and Vigilant, and had 56 M-901 ITV armored TOW carriers. Kuwait also had 4,000 Improved TOW missiles on order. Although this was a good mix of anti-tank weapons, the army only provided uncertain training and support effort for its anti-armor crews.

The artillery strength of the Kuwait Army included 36 M-109A2 self-propelled and 40 AMX Mark F-3 towed 155 mm howitzers, and approximately 16 old M-101 towed 105 mm howitzers. However, the army had no combat training in using such artillery beyond set-piece and firing-range exercises. Kuwait's surface-to-surface missile battalion had 12 FROG-7 launchers, but these had little more than symbolic importance.

Kuwait was gradually developing improved army land-based air defenses, although it had too many different types of weapons and was poorly trained in operating them. Kuwait had Soviet supplied SA-7s, SA-6s, and ZSU 23-4s, and two batteries of SA-8s. The US had refused to sell it the Stinger missile systems, but Kuwait had more SA-7s, Egyptian Sakr Eyes, and gun-missile defense systems on order. There were reports of additional orders for SA-6s and SA-8s, and that Kuwait had ordered Crotale or Sea Wolf light surface-to-air missile systems, but Britain was then reluctant to sell Kuwait a key system in service in the British navy because of the fear of loss of the details of the technology to the USSR.[120]

The Kuwaiti army had a massive $100 million military complex about twenty miles from Kuwait City. These facilities, however, owed more to political convenience than strategy, and an effort to maintain high living standards rather than military effectiveness. They were vulnerable to air attack, and over-centralized both the deployment of Kuwait's forces and their support functions in fixed locations. Kuwait's army had poor overall training, little coordination or effective command above the brigade level, and a maintenance and logistic system where paper work often took priority over military effectiveness. Further, Kuwait lacked the ability to deploy and sustain its forces in the field without foreign civilian support. Kuwait had concluded an agreement with Turkey to provide more advanced training, but this effort came too late to affect its military proficiency.[121]

The Kuwaiti Navy Before the Gulf War

Kuwait was just beginning to create a real navy when Iraq invaded. It had formed an 2,100 man naval force to replace its coast guard, but this force was completely dependent on foreign contractors for training, maintenance, logistics, and often actual operations. It was based at Ras al-Qulayah and Shuwaikh, and had recently acquired $29 million worth of new naval facilities. There were major civil ship repair facilities at Kuwait City's Shuwaikh harbor, including a 190 meter floating dock with a 35,000 DWT repair capability.[122]

The core of the Kuwait navy consisted of eight Lurssen guided missile patrol boats. Two of these boats were FPB-57s, and six were TNC-45s. They were each equipped with 76 mm OTO Melara guns, twin 40 mm guns, and four Exocet MM-40 missile launchers. It should be noted that these patrol boats had some important limitations common to virtually all GCC naval vessels. They lacked air defense capability, and while their voice communications were good, they could not be integrated into a data link exchange network. Crewing them also required nearly 60% of Kuwait's native naval manning.[123]

Kuwait received five 55-meter South Korean missile patrol boats beginning in August, 1987, which were based on Kuwait's offshore islands. The ships each had anti-ship missiles, helicopter pads, and a Hovercraft docking facility. The ships were not fully combat ready, but they did increase Kuwait's shallow water defense capability. Kuwait also had 47 small patrol craft, 4 modern British Cheverton LCTs, 3 LCUs, 3 LSUs, 4 tugs, 6 launches and some light coastal vessels and support craft. The Kuwaiti air force provided additional support in the form of Super Puma helicopters equipped with the Exocet missile system.

Finally, Kuwait had six SRN-6 Hovercraft, Exocet-capable SA 365N Dauphin II helicopters, 20 Magnum Sedan patrol boats, two Italian 18.4 meter patrol boats, two 20-meter Italian patrol boats, and more South Korean patrol boats on order. It was negotiating with the Netherlands to buy two Alkmaar-class mine hunters, and the Dutch Parliament had approved the loan of two such vessels until new production became available.

While this naval strength was reasonable for a small navy, it also required a manpower base of 5,000–8,000 men in uniform, or 3 to 4 times the manpower Kuwait actually possessed. Kuwait got around some of these requirements by being heavily dependent on foreign technicians, but overall readiness was poor.

The Kuwaiti Air Force Before the Gulf War

Kuwait's 2,200 man air force was slowly improving its effectiveness. The air force had roughly 70 combat aircraft and 18 armed helicopters. It had good basing facilities at Kuwait International Airport, Ahmed Al Jaber Air Base, and Ali Al Salem Air Base. Housing and other facilities were good.

Its combat strength included 30 A-4KU/TA-4KU attack fighters, some of which were being placed into storage to await the delivery of new F-18 multi-role fighters which Kuwait had ordered from the US.[124] The A-4s were adequate attack aircraft, but did not have air combat radars. They could only be used in dogfights where ground-based radars or Kuwait's Mirage F-1s guided them to a target. This made them hopelessly inferior to Iraq's modern fighters in air-to-air combat capability.

The air force had 24 new Mirage F-1BK/CK fighters and 12 Mark 64 Hawk COIN/trainer aircraft. Kuwait's air weapons inventory included AIM-9 Sidewinders, Matra Super R-530, and R-550 Magique air-to-air missiles—with AS-11 and AS-12 air-to-surface missiles, and 12 AM-39 air-to-ship missiles on order. Kuwait had also ordered the French SA-365N maritime attack system.

The Mirage F-1 aircraft proved hard to maintain, however, and Kuwait lost several of these aircraft in accidents. The radar of the Mirage F-1s had reliability problems and its 55 kilometer air intercept range proved too short to meet Kuwait's operational needs. As a result, Kuwait was forced to use its A-4 attack aircraft in a combat air patrol role when it needed to create an air defense screen. Further, Kuwait was so short of air force personnel that it contracted for Pakistani service and support crews.[125]

Kuwaiti training was adequate for interdiction and close air support missions against targets that lacked good ground-based air defenses, but was not suited for attacks on Iraqi forces. Kuwaiti pilots also had relatively limited air-to-air combat training, and were severely hampered by an inadequate air command and control system, and air warning and surveillance coverage. Little effort was made to develop a force that could maintain a high alert status or work with the army in effective combined operations. The Mirage F-1s did, however, maintain a limited alert status during the Iran-Iraq War.

These problems help explain why Kuwait ordered 40 US F/A-18 fighters in July 1985, at a cost of $1.9 billion. The sale also included 120 AIM-9 Sidewinder air-to-air missiles, 200 AIM-4 Sparrows, 40 AGM-84 Harpoon anti-ship missiles, and 300 Maverick AGM-65G anti-ship/anti-hard point missiles. US approval of this sale, however, only came after a bitter fight between the Reagan Administration and Congress. In order for the Administration to win approval of the sale, Kuwait had to give up its effort to order 200 IR Maverick AGM-65D anti-tank missiles. Kuwait also had to agree to base the F/A-18s only in Kuwait, not to acquire a refueling capability, and to exchange one A-4KU for every F/A-18 delivered to Kuwait.

This compromise left Kuwait with limited levels of munitions stocks for its new aircraft, and without an advanced anti-tank weapon for the F/A-18. Further, the F/A-18s were not scheduled to begin delivery until January, 1992, and Kuwait was not scheduled to receive its active strength of 28 fighters and eight fighter trainers until June, 1993, and its remaining four attrition aircraft until after 1994. This drawn out delivery schedule meant increased turbulence and transition problems. At the same time, the F-18 sale promised to give Kuwait an advanced air defense/air attack fighter, and advanced munitions and support facilities which were standardized with those used by the US Navy and US Marines and which could significantly improve US over-the-horizon reinforcement capability.[126]

The Kuwait air force had nine transport aircraft, including one B-707-200, six C-130-30s, and two DC-9s.[127] The Air Force operated 46 helicopters. These included 23–30 SA-342K Gazelle attack helicopters, 23 of which were equipped with HOT. They also included 5–6 AS-332 Super Pumas equipped with Exocet, and 10–12 SA-330 Pumas. It had 6 AS-332F Super Pumas on order. The helicopter crews had moderate training and good foreign maintenance support.

Kuwait had a French designed, semi-automated air defense, control, and warning system, but it had only limited low altitude coverage of Iraq, Iran and the Gulf. It also had limited electronic warfare capability, and readiness and operational reliability, and Kuwait does not seem to have been able to take advantage of some of the computerized features of the system because of software and training problems. The Kuwaiti Air Force did benefit from data exchanges with the E-3As flying in Saudi Arabia, but the quality of the data links was uncertain. This system did not allow either Kuwaiti fighters or its surface-to-air missiles to react quickly and effectively enough to deal with Iranian or Iraqi intruders in Kuwait's air space.

In August 1990, Kuwait's Air Force had five batteries of Improved Hawk surface-to-air missiles with 24 twin launcher fire units, 12 SA-8 surface-to-air missile launcher units, and an unknown number of SA-7 and SA-14 man portable surface-to-air missiles. It also had 20 mm and 35 mm anti-aircraft guns, and may have had two Shahine batteries on order. Kuwait had serious problems in absorbing its more sophisticated surface-to-air missiles. This became clear in 1987, when efforts were made to re-site the missiles to defend against attacks by Iran's Silkworm missiles. It is unclear how many IHawk units were really combat-ready when Iraq invaded. The US refusal to sell Kuwait Stinger missiles in June, 1984, led Kuwait to delay the purchase of Hawk systems and buy some $327 million worth of light Soviet arms for its Army—none of which could be netted into an effective air defense system.

Kuwaiti Paramilitary Forces Before the Gulf War

Finally, Kuwait had separate National Guards, Palace Guards, and Border Guards, which were equipped with a total of 20 V-150 and 62 V-300

Commando armored personnel carriers. The National Guards were intended for civil control and had little military capability. The Ministry of the Interior ran special political and anti-terrorist police forces, and was responsible for internal intelligence and security. These security and intelligence forces had a poor reputation before Iraq's invasion, and their actions after Kuwait's liberation indicate that this reputation was justified.

8

Rebuilding Kuwait's Forces
Following the Gulf War

Kuwait did not wait for its liberation to begin rebuilding its military forces. It began to rebuild its air force and army during Desert Shield, and Kuwaiti land and air units played a significant role in Desert Storm and Kuwait's liberation. The Gulf War has, however, forced Kuwait to accept the fact that it cannot obtain security through political or financial means, that the GCC cannot provide it with security against major regional powers like Iran and Iraq, and that it is dependent on outside powers—mainly the US—for its security.

The Gulf War has also forced Kuwait to drastically rethink its defense plans and force structure, and to recognize a number of major challenges that will shape its future strategic position. On the one hand, it has become brutally clear that Kuwait must develop combat effective forces to deter Iraq and Iran, to demonstrate that it can maintain its sovereignty, and to show the US and its neighbors in the Southern Gulf that it can be a true partner in meeting external threats. There is no way that Kuwait can return to its pre-war policy of relying on a combination of diplomatic maneuvering, "aid" to potential threats, and a limited deterrent force for its security.

On the other hand, it is equally clear that Kuwait faces the following major strategic problems in developing the military forces it needs for the future:

- There is no way to overcome the geographic fact that Kuwait has no strategic depth and will remain highly vulnerable to Iraq and Iran as long as these nations have major military forces.
- It no longer is seeking force levels of 40,000 men, However, its present goal of creating a roughly 30,000 man force will not allow it to defend against an Iraqi or Iranian attack, and may be too large to be practical. Further, its refusal to offer full citizenship to the children of immigrants, or Bidoon, regardless of background and loyalty, deprives it of a critical source of manpower.

- It has acted on the conviction that its military forces must be purged of any elements that are not fully loyal to Kuwait, leading Kuwait, rightly or wrongly, to reject about half of its pre-invasion manpower.
- There is no near-term possibility that Saudi Arabia and the other GCC states could provide the land and air strength necessary to halt an Iraqi attack before it seizes Kuwait, or provide the kind of air and missile defense screen necessary to defend Kuwait against Iran.
- Egypt and Syria are unlikely to provide an adequate Arab military force under financial and political conditions that Kuwait finds acceptable, and may be unable to project effective military power this far from their home bases.
- The US cannot project armored and mechanized forces large enough to defeat an Iraqi attack without either a month of strategic warning, or a combination of prepositioned equipment, forward deployed forces, and constant training. At the same time, the effective use of US air power requires access to both Saudi and Kuwaiti bases, prepositioned munitions, and a fully modern and interoperable combination of sheltered air bases, surface-to-air defenses, and C⁴I systems.

Since 1992, Kuwait has pursued a combination of restructuring and expanding Kuwaiti forces, encouraging US prepositioning, stronger military ties to Saudi Arabia, and discussions with other Arab states. It has had some important successes in implementing this policy and in rebuilding its military forces, but it still faces major challenges.

The Problem of Kuwaiti Military Manpower

The most serious challenge Kuwait faces in rebuilding its military capabilities is manpower. Chart Sixteen shows the trends in Kuwaiti military manpower. It is clear that Kuwait has always had a limited manpower pool to draw upon. Kuwait now has a total of about 102,000 males between the ages of 13 and 17, 78,400 between the ages of 18 and 22, and 140,800 between the ages of 23 and 32. Kuwait talks about a conscription system, but this amounts more to short term volunteers rather than real conscripts. Half of its manpower is still volunteer.[128]

Further, Kuwait made its problems worse by failing to recruit most of the members of the resistance into its armed forces after the liberation. It has not attempted to enlist most of its Shi'ite citizens, and has purged its army of many of the 10,000 Bedouins, who were not full Kuwaiti citizens after the war—even though some fought against the Iraqis or in the resistance. As a result, Kuwait's remaining pool of males of military age is only about 160,000 men.[129]

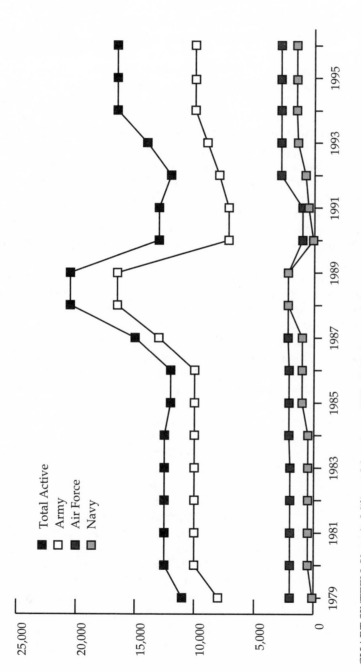

CHART SIXTEEN Kuwait: Military Manning—1979–1996. *Source:* Adapted by Anthony H. Cordesman from various editions of the IISS, *Military Balance*, the JCSS, *Military Balance in the Middle East,* and material provided by US experts.

In early 1996, Kuwait had a total force of only 16,600 actives, including 1,600 foreign personnel, 1,000 men in the central staff and 600 Emiri Guards. It claimed to have some 23,700 reserves, with one month of annual training, but only a small portion of this total seemed to be organized into reserve forces. Much of this manpower was composed of full citizens. However, there were large numbers of Bangladeshi, and Kuwait had to bring back some of the Bedouin whom it had fired from the armed forces to make up roughly one-third of this total. There is no sign of a draft.[130]

There were reports during 1991–1994 that Kuwait faced serious morale and leadership problems among its officers. According to these reports, some officers believe their senior commanders were often promoted purely for family and political reasons and deserted in the face of the enemy when Iraq attacked. Some feel the royal family ignored those who fought in the resistance, and has allowed post-war contracts to be awarded on the basis of favoritism and corruption. They also question the government's efforts to study what went wrong and learn from the lessons of the war.

Things have improved, however, since the period immediately after the liberation. In April, 1991, a group of senior officers sent the Emir a letter calling for the investigation and dismissal of Defense Minster Sheik Nawaf al-Ahmad al Sabah for failing to mobilize, for pulling forces back from the border shortly before the invasion, for ordering the Kuwaiti tanks in the border area not to fire on the advancing Iraqi troops, and for fleeing the country without giving orders to Kuwait's forces once the war had begun. They also called for the investigation of Interior Minister Sheik Salem Sabah al-Salem for taking no action to provide suitable warning and internal security measures. The Emir dealt with this situation by making Nawaf Minister of Social Affairs and Labor, but he also made al-Salem the new Minister of Defense.[131]

In January 1992, the government faced serious protests by junior and mid-grade officers. They demanded the resignation of up to 100 military officers and defense personnel, including 20 generals and a number of members of the royal family. Some 14 officers were retired, but this was not sufficient for military or public opinion. While the new Minister of Defense, Sheik Ali Salem Sabah al-Salem was able to improve his relations with some of the military, he was rotated out of his position in 1994 because of his conflict with the National Assembly over the size and control of arms purchases. The royal family was also forced to replace Kuwait's chief of staff, Major General Jabir al-Khalid Al Sabah with Major General Ali al-Mu'min in the summer of 1993. General Al Sabah had been chief of staff during the Iraqi invasion, and had also been blamed for Kuwait's unpreparedness.[132]

US military officers who have participated in joint planning efforts and exercises with Kuwait believe that the Kuwaiti forces now have much stronger leadership, that the morale of Kuwaiti forces has steadily improved since early 1994, and that the morale of the Kuwait officer corps is now relatively high. They believe the joint Kuwaiti-US response to Iraq's movements in 1994 and 1995 has done much to convince the Kuwaiti military that they can serve a vital role in defending Kuwait in the future.

The quality of Kuwait's manpower intake into enlisted ranks has also improved since the Iraqi build up on Kuwait's border. Kuwait is taking in about 1,500 men per year, with 750 volunteers and 750 coming from the national service program. Kuwait is getting more volunteers of a higher quality, but 1,500 men a year is not enough to meet its force goals. Kuwait's mix of "draftees" and volunteers presents problems, however, because so many citizens are rich and therefore hard to recruit. Further, the armed services cannot reject low quality volunteers and draftees because of objections by the National Assembly.

Kuwait no longer uses large numbers of Palestinians and Jordanians to staff the Ministry of Defense's technical and support function, including some aspects of contracting and procurement, because of the Gulf War. However, Kuwait's military manpower is so low that many services still have to be contracted to civilians, including many Asians. Kuwait remains heavily dependent on foreign personnel for its technical, service and logistic support, and maintenance and training, and US, British, and French military and contractor support missions. This limits Kuwaiti sustainment and redeployment capability in war time.[133]

The Challenge of Re-equipping Kuwaiti Forces

Kuwait faces problems in re-equipping its forces that are almost as serious as its manpower problems. It must make up for its wartime losses, increase its holdings of major equipment, and seek to obtain superior technology as a partial compensation for Iraqi or Iranian military superiority. It faces major uncertainties as to how much of the equipment Iraq seized and then returned can ever be used again, and it almost certainly will not be able to afford its initial weapons procurement plans. At the same time, it must: (a) seek to make its equipment interoperable with that of US and Saudi forces—its major sources of reinforcement, (b) deal with the political problem of allocating arms sales in ways that encourage external support from other powers like Britain, France, and Russia, and (c) seek to improve interoperability and standardization with its other GCC allies at a time when they show little real interest in these issues.[134]

Iraq stole some 9,000 major items of military equipment from Kuwait during the invasion. Kuwait has only had mixed success in recovering this equipment—although it sometimes has had more success than it initially expected.[135] In early 1992, Sheik Ali Sabah Al Sabah—then Minister of Defense—stated that Iraq would not give back the equipment, and that, in any case, Kuwait could not use equipment the Iraqis had damaged or worn out in combat. He accused Jordan of working with Iraq to ensure that Iraq can use the IHawks that it took from Kuwait, and indicated that Kuwait would reequip its forces on the basis of British, Kuwaiti, and US studies of Kuwaiti security needs.[136]

Shortly thereafter, the current Kuwaiti Deputy Chief of Staff, Brigadier General Jaber Al Sabah, stated that Iraq had agreed to return all captured equipment by the summer of 1992, and that this would include 68–83 Chieftain and 67 Vickers MBT-1 tanks, many Soviet BMP-2 armored fighting vehicles, 23 M-109A3 155 mm howitzers, 12 120 mm mortars, hundreds of trucks, 11 aircraft, four helicopters, and a number of small craft and patrol boats.[137]

General Al Sabah also indicated that

- Iraq was actively testing its captured IHawks;
- Some of the A-4s Iraq had captured had been so damaged that they had to be flown back to Kuwait in slings;
- Six Mirage F-1s had been declared missing or destroyed,
- Four Hawk trainers were returned in bad condition;
- A returned C-130 had been seriously damaged, and
- The patrol boats Iraq returned to Kuwait had been damaged so severely that they had to be returned by land.[138]

Many of the tanks Iraq returned came back without their fire control systems. The howitzers needed a major rebuild, and the aircraft and helicopters were missing some of their navigation equipment. Further, in early 1995, Kuwait indicated that it still had not received 15 Kuwaiti FROG rockets, 215 Soviet-made armored personnel carriers, 55 M-901 armored personnel carriers, 4,000 TOW anti-tank guided missiles, three portable anti-aircraft systems, and thousands of trucks. Since these are all items that are of value to Iraq in rebuilding its forces, it seems doubtful that Kuwait will now see their return.[139]

In short, Kuwait has been confronted with having to either equip its forces from the ground up, or rely heavily on worn and damaged equipment which does not give it a technical edge over Iran and Iraq. It also faces the problem that some of its key potential suppliers are also interested in future sales to Iraq—a factor that already has led Kuwait to begin putting pressure on Russia and France to choose between the Kuwaiti and Iraqi markets.[140]

9

Kuwait's Land Forces
Since the Gulf War

Kuwait's army manpower totaled about 10,000 regulars in mid 1996.[141] The Army was organized into two active mechanized brigades, two active armored brigades, one Emiri Guards Brigade, one reserve brigade, one active artillery brigade, and one engineer brigade. It also had a 1,000 man commando battalion. These Kuwaiti "brigades," however, only had about 1,000–1,500 men, and one armored brigade was still equipped largely with "Humvees" and was not scheduled to receive its full armor until 1997. The total manning of the Kuwait Army was equivalent to about one Western brigade slice.[142] The trends in Kuwaiti Army manning are shown in Chart Sixteen.

Kuwaiti has set a goal of creating four active, full brigades, but a number of experts believe this is not possible. These experts believe that Kuwait can create two fully manned and well equipped armored brigades, and two other brigades which mix active manning with a rapidly mobilizable reserve. They also assert that such a force would be large enough to help deter any sudden Iraqi incursions and to delay Iraqi forces long enough for US air and land power to begin to be effective in halting a major Iraqi attack.

Kuwaiti Army Modernization and Expansion

The trends in Kuwaiti Army equipment are shown in Charts Seventeen and Eighteen. These charts show the slow rate of build-up before the Gulf War, the devastating impact of the Gulf War, and the Army's post-war recovery. Kuwait has, however, had to make major cuts in the army re-equipment plans it developed immediately after the Gulf War. Kuwait initially considered ordering some 700 main battle tanks, and matching numbers of armored infantry fighting vehicles, artillery weapons and other systems. As has been explained earlier, however, the National Assembly has placed growing limits on Kuwaiti arms purchases, and Kuwait has had to adopt considerably more modest goals.

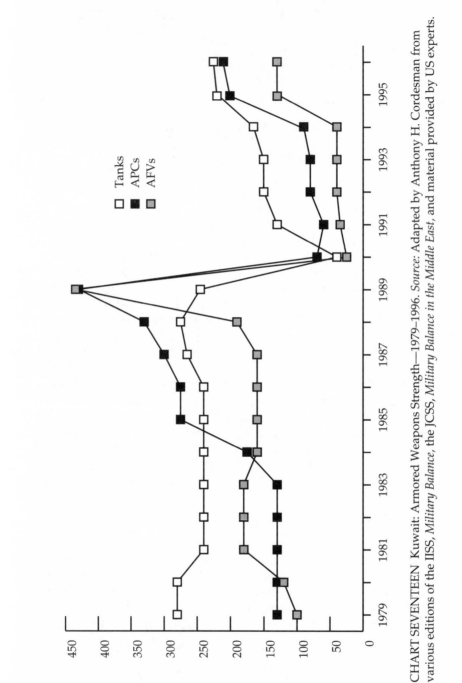

CHART SEVENTEEN Kuwait: Armored Weapons Strength—1979–1996. *Source:* Adapted by Anthony H. Cordesman from various editions of the IISS, *Military Balance,* the JCSS, *Military Balance in the Middle East,* and material provided by US experts.

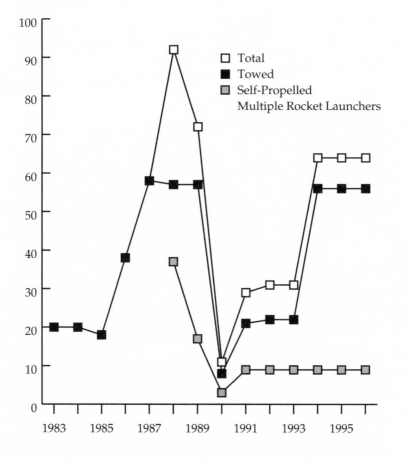

CHART EIGHTEEN   Kuwait: Artillery Weapons Strength—1979–1996.
Source: Adapted by Anthony H. Cordesman from IISS, *Military Balance,*
the JCSS, *Military Balance in the Middle East,* and material provided by US
experts.

Kuwait's operational tank strength now seems to include 85 Yugoslav
M-84s, out of a total of 150. The rest are in storage because of manpower
problems and a lack of spare parts. The M-84s tanks are variations of the
T-72 with mediocre armor and sighting systems, and inferior ammunition, but have fire control systems superior to many early-model T-72s
including those T-72s currently in Iraq's inventory. There are reports that
Kuwait is seeking Russian assistance in bringing the M-84s up to the standard of improved late-model T-72s by adding major improvements in fire
control capability and improved ammunition for the 125 mm gun.[143]

Kuwait had 16 M-1A2 tanks in early 1996, which were part of a $4.5 bil-
lion order for 218 M-1A2 US-made Abrams tanks. These tanks will allow
Kuwait to equip two armored brigades with first-line equipment that is
far superior to any tanks in Iranian and Iraqi service and which are standardized with the tanks in US and Saudi forces. Deliveries of the M-1s
began in August, 1995, and are to be completed by 1997. The first 16 tanks
joined Kuwait's Shaheed, or "Martyrs Brigade."

At the same time, Kuwait has given up plans to replace its low-qual-
ity, Yugoslav-supplied M-84 tanks with 100–150 more M-1A2s. Even the
two armored brigades it is already planning to equip with M-1A2s are
only two-thirds manned, and Kuwait does not have the money to fund
a large purchase of more M-1A2s. As a result, it will probably have to
continue to equip two brigades with the M-84 and other Russian combat
equipment.[144] Some experts believe it will equip its two active brigades
with US and British equipment and its two mobilizable brigades with
Yugoslav and Russian equipment.

Kuwait's order for its M-1 tanks also illustrates the problems Kuwait
and other Southern Gulf states have when they hold weapons trials and
attempt to choose equipment on the basis of operational merit, rather than
politics and technical claims. The losing seller or seller nation inevitably
cries fowl and resorts to politics.

Kuwait conducted a comparative test of the US M-1A2 and British
Challenger 2 tanks in 1992. The US M-1A2 proved to have the advantage, with a top speed of 65 km/h versus 50 for the Challenger 2, and
superior braking. It scored three hits out of three at 2,000 meters versus
one out of three for the Challenger 2, 10 hits versus eight at 4,000
meters, six hits firing on a slope versus two, and four hunter-killer hits
in 32 seconds out of four fired versus three hits out of four in 66 seconds. Similarly, the M-2 Bradley out-scored the Warrior with a 90% hit
on the move score versus 16% for the Warrior, and three TOW hits out
of three firings versus one for the Warrior. The results of these trials
became so controversial, however, that Kuwait made a political decision to buy the Warrior fitted with the Delco LAV-25 two man turret,
and to balance its future purchases between the US, Britain, and France
in an effort to ensure it will receive reinforcements from both the US
and Europe.[145]

Kuwait's other armored vehicle strength seems to include 46 BMP-2s
and 76 BMP-3s, about 153 M-113s, 40 Fahd APCs, 6 M-577s, some
armored mortar carriers, and roughly 20 special purpose and armored
engineering vehicles. Kuwait may have 10–15 BDRMs and some Ferret
and Saladin armored fighting vehicles in storage. These holdings represent too many types of equipment for a small force, and it is clear that
Kuwait urgently needs new modern infantry fighting vehicles.

Kuwait is attempting to solve this problem by purchasing 254 British Warrior AIFVs ($918 million), but it has given up plans to standardize on the Warrior, and buy the 450–600 it once considered.[146] Deliveries began in mid-1995, and about 20 had been delivered as of August. A total of 136 of the Warriors will have thermal imaging vision, Delco LAV-25 turrets with 25 mm guns, two armored TOW anti-tank missile launchers, and ACE. They will be used in the two regiments equipped with the M-1s.

The other Warriors will include recovery vehicles which will tow support trailers, command posts, and repair vehicles. Some will have high mobility support trailers and special support equipment. Kuwait has bought modern simulation and training systems for its Warriors, but it will take two years for Kuwaiti forces to get full delivery of its order and fully convert to the new system.[147]

Kuwait is filling out its armored strength by buying 125 M-113 APCs, 40 BMP-2 and 20 BMP-3s. The BMPs will be used along with the M-84s in the Sixth Mechanized Liberation Brigade. These sales were part of the defense agreement Kuwait and Russia signed in November, 1993. The agreement provides for up to $763 million in sales, and requires a Russian reinvestment in offset programs of at least $228.9 million.[148] It is considering buying an armored system with a Chieftain body and a Piranha turret with TOW missiles.

Kuwait also plans to procure up to 263 wheeled armored vehicles at a cost of $385 to $462 million. It is evaluating an initial purchase of 80–130 vehicles for the Emir's guard, and the candidates include the Swiss Piranha, Styer-Daimler Pandur, 6 x 6, Textron LAV-300 6 X 6, and Russian BTR-80. Many will be equipped with a LAV-25 25 mm turret or a Cockerill Mark IIIA1 90 mm gun. Other purchases will include 108–110 mortar carriers to provide fire support for Kuwait's mechanized forces and new Warriors and BMP-3s. The main candidates are the Turkish FMC-Nurol M-113 with an armor mortar turret or a French 120 mm rifled mortar, and the British AMS 120 mm mortar on a United Defense vehicle. Kuwait is also examining the purchase of a Piranha with the Blazer turret, equipped with a 25 mm gun and VSHORADS missile launcher.[149]

These plans may end up giving Kuwait too many types of vehicles from too many countries and manufacturers, and too many light armored vehicles that cannot directly engage Iraqi heavy armored forces in combat. Kuwait does need light armored vehicles to deal with infiltration of its borders and other internal security missions, for air defense, and other special purpose uses. Rather it might do better by giving priority to standardizing on the Warrior.

Kuwait's surviving anti-tank weapons and new orders include large numbers of TOW and HOT anti-tank guided weapons, and at least 200 Carl Gustav 84 mm rocket launchers. Kuwait is evaluating purchase of the Milan 3 man-portable anti-tank weapon and has bought 1,015 TOW-2B missiles for its LAV-25 equipped armored vehicles.[150]

In early 1996, Kuwait's artillery strength included 22 M-109A2 self-propelled 155 mm howitzers, some M-56 and M-101 towed 105 mm howitzers, some 122 mm, 130 mm, and 152 mm weapons that seem to have been captured from Iraq, and a few multiple rocket launchers. Kuwait had 18 GIAT GCT AuF-1 towed and 16 AMX-13 AuF-3 self-propelled 155 mm artillery weapons in storage.[151]

Kuwait is establishing a new artillery regiment with 24–36 155 mm self-propelled howitzers and has the goal of building up a force of 100 155 mm weapons. It has had to reduce its original plans for major orders of new self-propelled artillery weapons, but is considering the purchase of 24 more 155 mm artillery systems. It is considering purchase of the US M-109A6 Paladin, the South African G-6, the British AS-90, and a Chinese weapon.[152]

It is studying an upgrade of its M-109 155 mm self-propelled howitzers to the M-109A6 Paladin improvement package or is considering the use of the VSEL AS90 155 mm turret. Kuwait is also attempting to sell its Auf-1s and replace them with the Giat Caesar 52 155 mm self-propelled or 155 TR towed weapon, and is considering a GIAT offer to modernize its AuF-3s.[153]

Kuwait ordered the Loral MLRS in 1989, but had to cancel the order because of its price. It has ordered 27 Russian BM 30 9A52-2 Smerch multiple rocket launchers, with a range of 70 kilometers, and had 9 in service in early 1996. These weapons are intended to equip three multiple launcher batteries in a separate regiment. Kuwait is currently integrating the Smerch, an effective long-range system, into its forces. As of yet, however, Kuwait lacks the ability to provide long-range targeting and battle management systems to make effective use of the weapon.

Kuwait is reported to be considering the purchase of the Russian SS-200 ground-to-ground missile, and/or Sakr-36 and Fatih rocket launchers from Egypt.[154] Kuwait is also considering the purchase of a UAV for artillery targeting and surveillance purposes.

Kuwait's surviving army air defenses include SA-7s, SA-14s, ZSU-23-4s and some 14.5 mm and 20 mm light anti-aircraft guns. Kuwait ordered 48 Shorts Starburst manportable anti-aircraft missile fire units and 300 missiles in October, 1994. Kuwait's air defense brigade will use the Starburst for air base defense and defending key strategic sites. Kuwait is considering additional purchases of the Starburst or the Mistral Atlas missile for deployment on "Humvee" 4 × 4 vehicles. Training to use the Starburst was underway in Belfast in July 1995. Kuwait is also considering the purchase of four batteries of mobile air defense systems. The candidates include the ADATS, Roland-3 with

VT-1 missiles, Alenia Aramais, and AdSAMS which fires the Aim-120 AMRAAM missile.[155]

Kuwait has placed additional orders with the US, many of which will strengthen its armored warfare capabilities. These include 46 M-88 tank recovery vehicles, 52 M-577 command post carriers, 230 M-1064 mortar carriers, 1,178 machine guns, 967 SINCGARS digital radio systems, 132 M-998 troop and cargo carriers, 460 heavy equipment carriers, 130,000 rounds of tank ammunition, and small arms ammunition. Kuwait also plans to order up to 700 unarmored "Humvee" troop carriers and large numbers of 2.5 and 5 ton support vehicles.[156]

Kuwaiti Army Readiness and Warfighting Capability

It will be at least three to five years before Kuwait can obtain delivery of all the equipment it now has on order, absorb it into its force structure, and provide suitable training. It also needs to create the dedicated support, maintenance, and logistic capabilities needed to fight effectively against first-line Iraqi forces. In terms of basing, the Kuwaiti army must rebuild its military complexes at virtually every level, although many buildings were left intact. This task involves expenditures of at least $275 million to repair all 11 of Kuwait's military bases.[157]

Equipment and basing problems are only part of the challenge Kuwait faces in creating effective land forces. Although the Kuwaiti army is improving, it still has a long way to go. Despite US and British training, Kuwait's restructured land forces still lack effective military capability in maneuver warfare, cannot fight effectively at night, do not have the ability to conduct independent artillery action, and are unable to fight intensive armored combat.

The army's movements to the border to oppose the Iraqi build-up in late 1994 indicated that Kuwait's ground forces still move too slowly, have trouble moving as a cohesive force, and lack the ability to deploy and sustain its forces in the field without foreign civilian support. However, the Kuwaiti army has made a major improvement in its readiness and combined arms training and performed well in command post and field training exercises in 1995 and 1996, and with US and Saudi units in the Peninsular Shield exercises in 1996.[158]

Some of the army's problems should also be sharply reduced once it has time to absorb its new equipment orders. Several realities, however, will not change:

- Kuwait cannot solve its manpower problems without broadening its recruiting base and some form of much more comprehensive conscription. Unless Kuwait takes major new initiatives to increase its military manpower, it will always have "hollow" forces.

- Second, Kuwait still over-emphasizes weapons and under-emphasizes support, sustainability, readiness, maneuver capability, training, and joint operations. Like most Southern Gulf forces, it emphasizes the symbolic value of large purchases of modern hardware over integrated and balanced war-fighting capability.

- Third, Kuwait is taking delivery on only enough modern armored equipment to match one heavy Republican Guards division. The Kuwaiti equipment will be qualitatively superior, but cannot provide Kuwait with more than a limited self-defense capability to deal with low-intensity land warfare in its border area. This equipment also will not be fully standardized with the equipment in US or Saudi forces. The rest of Kuwait's equipment will consist of low-grade armor which may do as much to kill its crews in intensive combat with first-line Iraqi armor as to kill the enemy, and there is little current prospect that Kuwait can replace this mix of low-grade tanks and OAFVs before the year 2005. This may not be as critical a problem as it appears, though, because it is unclear whether Kuwait really has the manpower to support a land force larger than two first-line active armored brigades. Kuwait's current land force procurement plans do, however, violate common sense to the extent that they fail to use Kuwait's wealth to buy the superior technology it needs to make up for its limited manpower.

- Finally, Kuwait will always be the single most vulnerable Gulf state. Kuwait City is within a few hours drive of the Iraqi border, and Kuwaiti population centers could be held hostage in any conflict. US and Gulf air and land power would then have to take such hostages into account. The US can improve its prepositioning capability and reaction times, but cannot remain in place in Kuwait. This makes the improvement of the Kuwaiti Army, and the development of Kuwait forces that can deter and delay an Iraqi defense a critical military priority.

10

Kuwait's Naval Forces
Since the Gulf War

Kuwait faces equal problems in restructuring its navy.[159] Chart Sixteen shows the trends in Kuwait naval manpower and the impact of the Gulf War. The Kuwaiti Navy had about 1,500 men in its naval forces in early 1996, including its Coast Guard. Kuwait's naval officers are trained by the British Kuwait Defense Group, although a few cadets are to be trained in France and the crews of its French-made ships are being trained at sea by Navfco. Kuwait is also training an additional 100 combat divers, including mine clearers.[160]

Kuwait's naval forces are based largely at El Adami and Shuwaikh. Kuwait has signed a contract to rebuild and expand its main naval base at Qalayah near Mina Sud, about 100 kilometers south of Kuwait City, which Iraq destroyed in 1990. Kuwait has ordered a new Rockwell-Celsius Tech command center and communications system to replace the one destroyed during the war.

Kuwaiti Naval Strength and Equipment

As Chart Nineteen shows, Kuwait has a relatively small navy compared to other Gulf forces. Kuwait lost most of the 23 ships in its pre-war navy during the fighting in 1990. These losses included its main force of eight missile patrol boats. By early 1996, however, its navy had built back to a strength of six combatants. These ships include one FPB-57 missile patrol boat (the *Istiqlal*), and one TNC-45 missile patrol boat (the *Al Sanbouk*). Each of these two ships has one 76 mm OTO Melara gun, twin 40 mm guns, and four Exocet MM-40 missile launchers (2 twin launchers). The FPB-57 was fitted for minelaying. Kuwait also has four 150 ton OPV-310 class patrol boats built in Australia and armed with 20 mm guns.[161]

Sources differ on Kuwait's holdings of smaller patrol boats. According to one source, the Kuwaiti Navy had 17 small patrol boats from Britain's Cougar Marine, and 12 Simmoneau Standard inshore patrol craft.[162]

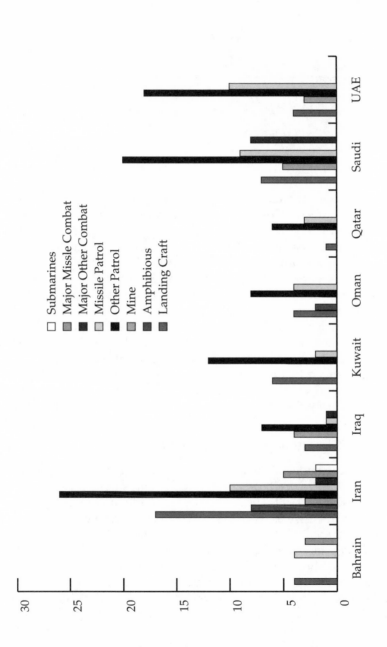

CHART NINETEEN Gulf Naval Ships by Category in 1996. *Source:* Adapted by Anthony H. Cordesman from the IISS, *Military Balance, 1995–1996,* and material provided by US experts.

Some of these boats were used by Kuwait's forces during the liberation of Kuwait. According to other sources, Kuwait had three catamarans, three 33' ultra-fast patrol boats, three 35' ultra-fast patrol boats, four 38' ultra-fast patrol boats, and four smaller ultra-fast patrol boats.[163]

Kuwait plans a further major expansion of its navy. The five South Korean Seagull class patrol boats Kuwait had ordered in 1986 were seized by Iraq and destroyed during the war. Kuwait, however, expects to take delivery on five more ordered in 1988, and commissioned two Australian 31.5 meter patrol boats in 1994.

Kuwait ordered eight Combattante-I 225-ton patrol boats on March 27, 1995. These ships are powered by MTU engines linked to waterjets, and each is armed with a 40 mm L70 gun and a M-621 20 mm gun. They will be equipped later with either the Aerospatiale MM-15 or British Sea Skua anti-ship missile and its associated radar, Matra Sadal or Shorts Seastreak air defense missiles, chaff launchers, and ESM/ECM systems. The missiles are expected to be ordered in 1996, and the ships are to be delivered in 1997–1999.[164]

Kuwait is likely to order four to six much larger 88–95 meter offshore missile vessels displacing 1,500 to 2,000 tons. These ships will be helicopter carriers with anti-ship and anti-air missiles. There are thirteen possible candidates for this program from nine countries, ranging from 1,350 to 2,200 tons.[165]

Other purchase plans include amphibious landing ships, naval helicopters with anti-ship missiles, and a wide range of new weapons systems and sensors. Kuwait is considering the purchase of sonar-based surveillance and detection systems to deal with the Iranian submarine threat, but seems to have given up plans to buy mine vessels and appears to be planning on foreign forces to deal with the mine warfare threat. It is considering the modernization and rebuilding of one TNC-45 missile patrol boat (*Al-Sanbouk*) and one FBP-57 missile patrol boat (*Istiqlal*). Both ships were captured by Iraq and survived, because they fled to ports in Iran and Bahrain during the war.[166]

Kuwaiti Naval Readiness and Warfighting Capability

If Kuwait completes all these orders, it will acquire a relatively large number of surface vessels for such a small country. Its navy may, however, be too large and be designed for the wrong missions. Kuwait will have made a major investment in surface vessels, designed largely to confront an Iraqi or Iranian surface threat in an area where the real threat may be from mines and anti-ship missile attacks on commercial ships, and where Kuwait's vessels may find it difficult to defend against Iranian and Iraqi aircraft and long-range land-based anti-ship missiles.

Kuwait might well have benefited more from investing the same money in mine warfare capabilities, armor, or increased air power.

The Kuwaiti Navy also has limited readiness and low prestige. It competes for resources with the Kuwaiti Coast Guard. This rivalry needs to be eliminated if Kuwait is to concentrate its limited resources in ways which create effective naval units.

In short, Kuwait is likely to remain dependent on the US and British navies for anything other than very low level contingencies. This situation will be compounded by the fact that both Iran and Iraq can attack virtually any maritime target in Kuwaiti waters with their long-range, land-based anti ship missiles, and the fact that the Iranian Navy and naval branch of the Iranian Revolutionary Guards Corps can attack quickly and with little warning. Kuwait has many of the same unique vulnerabilities at sea that it does on land.

11

Kuwait's Air Forces
Since the Gulf War

The trends in Kuwaiti air force manning are shown in Chart Sixteen, and the trends in Kuwait air strength are shown in Chart Twenty.[167] As might be expected, these trends have been heavily influenced by the impact of the Gulf War. Kuwait's air force now consists of about 2,500 men, with 76 combat aircraft and 16 armed helicopters. Its two main bases at Ali al-Salem (al-Jahrah) north of Kuwait City, and Ahmed al Jaber (al-Ahmadi) south of Kuwait City, suffered serious damage during the war, but are now operational, and repairs on the base at Ali al-Salem were completed in time to base Kuwait's new F/A-18s there by late 1992.[168]

Kuwaiti Air Force Equipment

Only a limited number of Kuwait's combat aircraft are fully operational. Kuwait has only eight operational Mirage F-1BK/CK fighters, out of a pre-war total of 23. It has 12 surviving armed Hawk 64 trainers, and 16 Shorts Tucanos organized as a counter-insurgency and training unit. These aircraft have only limited operational capability against an Iranian or Iraqi threat.

Kuwait has phased out its remaining 20 A-4KU/TA-4KU attack fighters it had left at the end of the Gulf War, out of a pre-war total of 30. Kuwait's A-4KU/TA-4KU attack fighters and F-1BK/CK fighters are on the market, and the operational aircraft of this type are used largely for sales demonstration purposes.[169]

As a result, Kuwait relies almost exclusively on its 40 F/A-18s, which are organized into a fighter/fighter ground-attack force. Kuwait took delivery of its first 12 F/A-18C/Ds in June, 1992, and delivery of its full order of 32 US F/A-18C and 8 F/A-18D fighters, AIM-9 Sidewinder air-to-air missiles, AIM-7F Sparrows, AGM-84 Harpoon anti-ship missiles, and Maverick AGM-65G anti-ship/anti-hard point missiles was completed by late 1994.

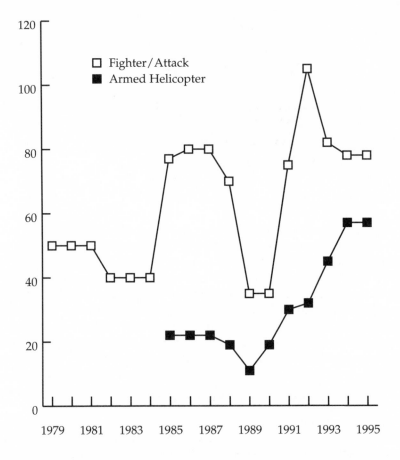

CHART TWENTY   Kuwait: Fixed Wing and Rotary Wing Combat Air Strength—1979–1996. *Source:* Adapted by Anthony H. Cordesman from IISS, *Military Balance,* the JCSS, *Military Balance in the Middle East,* and material provided by US experts.

Kuwait also completed its initial pilot training at the US Navy Air Station at Lenore, California, and began joint F/A-18 pilot training with US Navy pilots in Kuwaiti air space in March, 1993. Kuwait, however, is still well short of its goal of 1.5 trained aircrew per aircraft, and has a critical shortage of pilots. According to some reports, it had only 12 pilots for its F/A-18s in 1996.[170]

Kuwait began to make use of its F/A-18s during the border crisis of October, 1994. The Kuwaiti Air Force carried out joint exercises with US forces against targets only five kilometers from Iraq's forward deployed forces. The Kuwaiti Air Force also remained on continuous alert during the crisis. Twelve F/A-18s were kept loaded with either eight Mark 82 500 pound bombs or 20 Rockeyes. These aircraft were also armed with two AIM-9s and two AIM-7Fs, and some other F/A-18s were armed with Maverick.[171]

In early 1995, the Kuwaiti air force had two squadrons with a total active in-country strength of 31 F/A-18Cs and 7 F-18Ds (one F/A-18C and one F/A-18D are kept in the US for testing purposes). These squadrons included the 9th and 25th squadron. Both squadrons were capable of both attack and air defense missions, but one squadron trained 60% for the attack mission while the other trained 60% for the air defense mission. Both squadrons were deployed at Al Jaber Air Base, along with 24 USAF A-10s from the 23rd Wing (home-based at Pope Air Force Base).[172]

This is a very limited operational force for a nation as vulnerable as Kuwait, and Kuwait needs to expand and modernize its air force in several other ways. It needs to acquire more modern, high-capability fighters, to reach a decision regarding purchase of an airborne warning aircraft, to modernize its training and transport aircraft, to modernize its helicopter fleet and provide an attack helicopter capability. Moreover, Kuwait needs to establish at least one additional air base as far to the south as possible, a modern C⁴I/BM system, and an advanced integration land-based air defense system. Kuwait cannot accomplish all of these tasks in the near future, but it is making progress in a number of areas.

Buying and operating additional fighters will not be easy. Kuwait could not afford all of the new fighters it sought after the Gulf War, and had to cancel an option to buy 38 additional F/A-18s in 1992. It is, however, discussing longer term plans to order up to 35 more fighters, and may make an initial buy of 12 F/A-18C/D aircraft. Kuwait is also seeking to buy the AMRAAM air-to-air missile from the US, which would give it a major advantage over Iranian and Iraqi aircraft in beyond-visual-range combat capability and improve its interoperability with the Saudi and US air forces. Kuwait is also considering a possible buy of the Mirage 2000-5 multi-role fighter.[173]

Kuwait is seeking to fund such purchases by selling its remaining Skyhawks and Mirage F-1CTKs. Kuwait refurbished 15 of its Mirage F1CK/BKs with French aid by early 1995. It is seeking to sell these aircraft to Ecuador, but may continue to operate them if it cannot sell them or buy more F/A-18s.[174]

Kuwait is studying the possible purchase of airborne alert aircraft and/or maritime patrol aircraft. It may purchase the E-2C which provides both the capability to detect and intercept targets at long ranges and a maritime surveillance capability. The purchase would be an expensive one, however, and Kuwait may choose to rely on US and Saudi aircraft and aerostat mounted early warning radars.

Kuwait now operates a squadron of 6–12 British Hawk Mark 64 trainer-fighters, and 16 Short Tucano 312 trainer light attack aircraft (9 of which are operational). Kuwait is seeking to sell the Tucanos, which are now in the UK. It would like to buy Hawk 100 trainers, or at least upgrade its Mark 64s. Kuwait now has several C-130 transport aircraft, 1 DC-9, and 3 L-100-30s. Kuwait is considering the purchase of six more transports—probably C-130s and/or Shorts Sherpas.[175]

Many of Kuwait's helicopters were destroyed or seized during the war. The Air Force did, however, build back three operational helicopter squadrons by early 1995. These included 16 SA-342K Gazelle attack helicopters equipped with HOT anti-tank guided missiles, and 4 AS-332 Super Pumas and 8 SA-330 Pumas.

Attack helicopters offer Kuwait a way of providing rapid-reaction, anti-armor defenses that can help make up for its lack of strategic depth and defensive barriers. The SA-342Ks have not proved to be effective anti-tank helicopters, however, and the HOT missiles are being removed. Six of the aircraft are being armed with 20 mm cannons for border surveillance and counter-infiltration purposes and the others will be used as light attack-trainer helicopters.

As a result, Kuwait is seeking to purchase modern attack helicopters. It originally examined the purchase of 16–20 AH-64A Apache attack helicopters. The Apache offered a number of unique advantages to a nation like Kuwait. It is a highly lethal day-night, all-weather tank killer that can quickly reach any position in Kuwait, and which can evade or survive many of the mobile, short-range air defenses in Iraqi and Iranian forces. Its Hellfire missiles can be used against landing and small craft as well, and it can perform an armed reconnaissance mission with high survivability. At the same time, the purchase of 16 AH-64As had a cost of $692 million, and the AH-64A required roughly the same training and support effort as a modern fighter aircraft.[176]

These cost issues led Kuwait to examine other attack helicopter options, including the AH-1W, UH-60L Black Hawk, and Ka-50 Hokum. Kuwait decided on the UH-60L in July, 1995, and placed an order for 16 Blackhawk UH-60L helicopters at a cost of $461 million. The order also included four spare T700 General Electric engines, 500 Hellfire anti-armor missiles, 38 Hellfire launchers, 11,500 Hydra 70 rockets, 200 mm guns pods, and night vision devices. This order would save Kuwait nearly $200 million. It would also give Kuwait an attack helicopter with many of the anti-armor capabilities of the AH-64A, including a FLIR platform and a laser designator, which could be used in the armed transport mode. Kuwait is considering a follow-on purchase of the AH-64A or additional UH-60Ls in the mid-term, as well as the Hellfire II missile. It is also considering the purchase of AS-532 Cougar, Black Hawk, and IAR IAR-530 transport helicopters.[177]

The Black Hawk sale, however, ran into stiff opposition from the US military and is still pending approval. US officials are particularly concerned with Kuwait's request to outfit the Black Hawks with a missile-guiding designator and other equipment used only by US Special Forces units. Apparently, one of the chief concerns is that Kuwait's proximity to Iraq and its vulnerability to sudden attack could lead to the capture of this sensitive technology. Kuwaiti and US officials met in early December 1995, to find a compromise suitable to both sides. The Kuwaiti government is also awaiting the US government's decision regarding the possible sale of the Apache Longbow to Kuwait.[178]

Kuwait now has two air bases. Its fighters are located at its main Al Jaber Air Base. This base suffered extensive damage during the Gulf War from both Iraqi activity and US bombing that destroyed 22 of its 24 shelters. It has since been 75–80% restored, but it is clear that Kuwait needs a third air base to increase its survivability and dispersal, and the ability of US and other power projection forces to reinforce Kuwait. Kuwait has plans to create a new base in Southern Kuwait, but it is not clear when these plans will be funded.[179]

Kuwaiti Air Force Land-Based Air Defense and C⁴I/BM Systems

Kuwait developed a land-based air defense system with limited to moderate capabilities before the Iraqi invasion. This system used a Thomson-CSF C⁴I/BM system to control its fighters and IHawk missile units to integrate the data from a mix of AN/TPS-32, AR-3D, and TRS 2230 radars and two Litton AN/ASQ-73 systems to control its IHawks.[180] Most of the system was destroyed during the war, and Kuwait only had six fully operational batteries of short-range air defenses in early 1995. Each battery had one Skyguard radar, two Aspede surface-to-air missile fire units, and two twin 30 mm Oerlikon guns.[181]

As a result, Kuwait has had to create a new land-based air defense and C⁴I/BM system. Kuwait signed a $92 million contract with Hughes in December, 1992 to create a new land-based early warning system, refurbish an air operations center, and construct a new radar site. The first phase of the new system—the Preliminary Early Warning System (PEWS)—was accepted by the Kuwaiti Air Force in early 1996.[182] The system is shelter mounted, and integrates two of Kuwait's main search radars: a new AN/FPS-117 L-Band radar with a radome antenna and an existing French TSR-2100 Tiger S-Band radar at Kuwait City.

Work is also underway to integrate an airborne L-88 L-Band radar, mounted in an aerostat into the system and to correct high temperature operational environment problems with the FPS-117. Kuwait also ordered a long-range Thomson-CSF TRS 22XX S-Band three dimensional radar with a detection range of up to 450 kilometers in March, 1995. This radar will improve long-range surveillance at medium and high altitudes. Kuwait has set up a training center for the operators of its radars, and it is the first center in the Gulf to train operators in the use of high-definition color displays and voice-operated technology.[183]

Kuwait has also improved its cooperation in C⁴I/BM with the US and Saudi Arabia. Since 1994, the Kuwaiti Air Force has begun joint operations with US and Saudi aircraft that prepare it for joint air defense and air offensive operations with US and Saudi fighters. It can now operate as part of the US ATO system, and has digital links to the US Air Force AWACS and JSTARS aircraft. The Kuwaiti Air Force has shown that it can maintain an integrated air traffic control system over Kuwaiti air space and transmit low altitude radar data back to USAF command and control aircraft.

The real test of Kuwait's success, however, will be its ability to provide effective low-altitude radar coverage to supplement its medium-to-high-altitude radar systems, acquire a much more advanced Phase II C⁴I/battle management system, and deploy modern heavy surface-to-air missile defenses. Kuwait is now completing Phase II of its air defense system and the major competitors are Hughes and Westinghouse. It has been considering the purchase of low-altitude surveillance radars like the Thomson-CSF TRS-2140 S-Band radar.[184]

Kuwait is taking steps to acquire an advanced surface-to-air missile capability. Kuwait's main surface-to-air missile defenses will consist of five batteries of Patriot surface-to-air missiles, with 210 MIM-104 PAC-2 GEMs (Guidance Enhancement Missiles), ordered at a cost of $327 million. Kuwait has considered buying six new batteries of IHawk Phase III fire units and 342 MIM-23B Hawk missiles as well, but delayed this decision pending a study of possible reconstruction of the equipment for four IHawk batteries which Iraq returned after the war. According to some reports, Kuwait is also considering an order for Russian SA-10 or SA-12 (S-300PU) missiles.[185]

Kuwaiti Air Force Readiness
and Warfighting Capability

The Kuwaiti Air Force is making real progress, and US experts now rate Kuwaiti pilots as equivalent in training and skill to their US counterparts. Much will depend, however, on how the Kuwaiti Air Force manages its future arms purchases, whether it can improve its numbers of pilots and training ground crews, and whether it can evolve beyond the "knights of the air" level of most Gulf air forces.

The Kuwait Air Force needs a clearer strategic and tactical rationale and needs to be able to train and operate as an integrated force, rather than small groups of aircraft. It needs a clear concept of joint operations. It also faces the limitation that it cannot accomplish these goals in dealing with more than a low level threat unless it is interoperable with the Saudi and US air forces, can operate using modern USAF C^{4}I/BM systems, and has the option of extending its strategic depth by operating out of bases in Bahrain and Saudi Arabia.

It is not clear what degree of integration Kuwait can achieve with Saudi Arabia and Bahrain in creating a common air defense, maritime surveillance, and theater ballistic missile defense system. Full-scale computerized digital integration among all three countries is critical to providing effective air and maritime defense in the upper Gulf. This would give the Southern Gulf states an "edge" over Iran and Iraq, and effective interoperability with US air and naval forces.

It would be extremely desirable to develop such an integrated system on a GCC-wide basis. Kuwait's small size and air space, common border with Iraq, and proximity to Iran, all require Kuwait to have a survivable air defense and land and maritime surveillance system. No Kuwaiti-based system can provide such characteristics unless it is integrated into a Saudi system, preferably with close links to Bahrain, Qatar, and the UAE. At present, however, plans for improved integration are limited, and Saudi Arabia's new Peace Shield system would have to be redesigned to provide optical fiber links to other countries.

12

Kuwaiti Paramilitary
and Internal Security Forces

Kuwait has few paramilitary forces other than a National Guard. This force has an authorized strength of 5,000, although its actual strength is much lower. Kuwait does, however, have strong internal security forces. The Minister of Interior supervises Kuwait's security apparatus, which includes the Criminal Investigation Department (CID) and Kuwait State Security (KSS). These two agencies investigate internal, security-related offenses, in addition to the regular police.

Kuwaiti Security Measures

Although Kuwait has an elected National Assembly, it places tight controls on many aspects of political activity. Kuwait bans political parties, and associations that are not registered with the government. The government prevents unregistered human rights groups from holding public meetings. It also has a policy of preventing the return of stateless, Iraqi, and Palestinian people who have strong family ties to Kuwait, and its labor laws do not cover foreign-born domestic servants.

These security measures need to be kept in careful perspective. They have often been the subject of intense criticism by human rights organizations—particularly between 1991 and 1993, when the government drove many foreigners out of Kuwait and conducted security trials to punish those who had aided Iraq during its occupation of Kuwait. There is no doubt that there were many real abuses of human rights during this period. There is also no doubt that Kuwaiti internal security procedures have never met Western standards of human rights, rules of evidence, or police procedures.

Kuwait, however, has been the target of aggressive Iranian and Iraqi intelligence operations, and has had to deal with much more severe internal, security threats than the other Southern Gulf countries. From 1979 to the present, it has faced constant problems with Iranian intelligence operations inside Kuwait. During the Iran-Iraq War these took the form of aggressive sabotage, bombings, and assassination attempts.

Iraqi intelligence systematically infiltrated Kuwait during late 1989 and early 1990, building on intelligence networks which, in some cases, dated back to the early 1980s. Many foreign workers—including many Palestinians and Jordanians—did collaborate with the Iraqi occupying forces and this sometimes resulted in the torture, killing, or disappearance of Kuwaiti citizens.

The US State Department also reports that Kuwait has improved conditions in prisons and detention centers, extended the franchise to the sons of naturalized citizens, and invited the International Labor Organization (ILO) to Kuwait for consultations. It indicates that the Human Rights Committee of the National Assembly is playing a growing role in investigating important human rights abuses, and has recommended improvements in prison conditions.[186]

Criticism of Kuwait's internal security procedures must be tempered with the understanding that Kuwait faces very real problems. While Kuwait does not follow Western human rights practices, it also faces far more severe problems and threats than most Western governments. Further, Britain has been forced to adopt somewhat similar security practices in dealing with the situation in Northern Ireland, as did France when it attempted to deal with Algerian independence.

The Impact of the Kuwaiti Legal System

Like all Gulf states, the Kuwaiti legal system allows the government to deal with security cases differently from standard civil cases. The Constitution provides for the freedom from arbitrary arrest and detention, but security forces do not always respect these rights. Security forces in Kuwait City sometimes set up checkpoints where they may briefly detain individuals. Police officers must obtain arrest warrants from state prosecutors before making arrests, though in misdemeanor cases the arresting officer may issue them.[187]

Under the Penal Code, a suspect may not be held for more than four days without charge. Security officers sometimes prevent families from visiting detainees during this confinement. After four days, prosecutors must either release the suspect or file charges. If charges are filed, prosecutors may remand a suspect to an additional 21 days in detention. Prosecutors may also obtain court orders for further detention pending trial.[188]

Detention rules are different for cases involving state security. In such cases, prosecutors may hold a suspect in detention for six months, and a judge may authorize a longer confinement pending trial. After 21 days in detention, a defendant has the right to petition for his release in the State Security Court. If the judge denies the motion, the defendant may submit another appeal 30 days after the rejection. In general, cases go to trial between 20 and 30 days after arrest. The State Department reports that there is no evidence of long-term incommunicado detention, though there are about 30 detainees facing deportation, especially Iraqi citizens and the Bidoon, who have been in detention for more than a year. Approximately 1,850 people were in prison in 1994, of whom 400 are in pretrial detention.[189]

About 75 percent of the detainees face administrative deportation orders which the Ministry of Interior can issue arbitrarily. There are no trials for deportations and deportees do not have "due process." The Government may expel non-citizens, even those who have been long-term residents, if it considers them security risks. The Government may also expel foreigners if they are unable to obtain or renew work or residency permits. The State Department reports that the Government deported 122 Iraqis and nationals of countries that supported Iraq in the Gulf War (primarily Yemen and Jordan) in 1994, well below the 1993 level. The Government also routinely deported Iranians and other foreign nationals who have violated residency requirements or committed other offenses.[190]

The judicial system is also part of the internal security system. It is composed of the regular courts, which try criminal and civil cases, and the State Security Court, which tries cases of a security nature; and the Court of Cassation, which is the highest level of judicial appeal. During periods of martial law, the Emir may authorize military courts to try civilian defendants. There have been no martial-law trials since 1991. The Emir has the constitutional power to pardon or commute all sentences.[191]

Both defendants and prosecutors may appeal verdicts of the State Security Court to the Court of Cassation, but the appellate court may only determine whether the law was properly applied with respect to the sentence. The Court of Cassation cannot rule on guilt or innocence. Most security trials are public, as was the case in the 1994 trial of 14 persons accused in the foiled assassination plot against former President Bush. In June the State Security Court convicted 13 defendants and acquitted one. It sentenced six defendants to death and seven to prison terms ranging from six months to 12 years.

The State Department reports that this trial, like other security trials, did not meet internationally accepted standards with regard to an independent judiciary and the evidence required for proving criminal wrongdoing. It reports that the judges in martial-law courts have handed down several death sentences based on confessions apparently obtained under torture and that the courts later refused to reopen these trials. The sentences were, however, commuted to imprisonment ranging from 10 to 20 years. It also reports that the State Security Court ruled against excluding the confession of the 14 persons accused of attempting to assassinate former US President George Bush—despite allegations raised by the defense that the confessions were obtained by torture.

Freedom of Expression and Peaceful Dissent

Kuwait allows more freedom of expression than most other states in the Gulf and the Middle East, although it again has powerful legal tools to maintain internal security. The US State Department reports that several laws empower the Government to impose restrictions on the freedom of speech and the press, but the Government did not apply these laws in 1994. The State Department also reports that academics conduct their activities with no apparent censorship of their teaching, research, or writings, while subject to the same restraints as the media with regard to criticism of the Emir or Islam. Ordinary citizens are free to criticize the Government at public meetings and in the media.[192]

The government ended direct censorship in 1992. Journalists still, however, censor themselves, and the Press Law prohibits the publication of direct criticism of the Emir, official government communications with other states, and material that "might incite people to commit crimes, create hatred, or spread dissension among the people."[193]

Newspapers are privately owned and are free to publish material on many social, economic, and political issues. They frequently criticize government policies and officials, including the Prime Minister. Newspapers must, however, obtain an operating license from the Ministry of Information. This licensing power allows the Government control over the establishment of new publications. The law also stipulates that publishers may lose their license if their publications do not appear for six months. This "six-month" rule prevents publishers from publishing sporadically and is not used to suspend or shut down existing newspapers. Individuals must also obtain permission from the Ministry of Information before publishing any printed material, including brochures and wall posters. Foreign journalists are not censored and the Government permits them open access to the country.

The Government owns and controls the radio and television companies, although the Middle East Broadcasting Company and Egyptian television transmit to Kuwait without censorship. The government does not inhibit the purchase of satellite dishes. Citizens with such devices are free to watch a variety of programs, including those broadcast from Israel.[194]

The Ministry of Information has a Censorship Department that reviews all books, films, videotapes, periodicals, and other imported publications.

In practice, such censorship is sporadic and aimed mostly at morally offensive material; however, political topics may be censored. The General Organization of Printing and Publishing controls the printing, publishing, and distribution of informational material.[195]

There are additional limits on political activity and legal controls that allow the government to maintain internal security. All non-governmental organizations (NGOs) are illegal unless they obtain a license from the Ministry of Social Affairs and Labor. The Government uses its power to license as a means of political control. The Ministry has registered over 55 NGOs, including professional groups, bar associations, and scientific bodies. These groups receive government subsidies for their operating expenses. They must also obtain permission from the Ministry before attending international conferences. Since 1985 the Ministry has issued only two licenses, including one in 1994 to the Union of Kuwaiti Womens' Groups, which is headed by the wife of the Crown Prince. The Ministry has not approved other requests for licenses on the grounds that previously established NGOs already provide services similar to those proposed by the petitioners.

There are many private organizations whose activities are largely ignored by the government. However, the Cabinet issued a decree in 1993 ordering all unregistered NGOs to cease such activities, and no organization has challenged this decree in court. In September, 1994, the Ministry of Interior ordered three unregistered NGOs to vacate the offices that they had established in unused government buildings. The NGOs complied with the order. In banning these unregistered NGOs, the government sought to dissolve groups whose efforts were not coordinated with a government committee working for the release of missing persons presumed to be held in Iraq. The Government viewed such groups as politically unacceptable.[196]

Treatment of Foreign Labor

Kuwaiti Labor Law does apply to Kuwaiti nationals, but virtually all Kuwaiti national either work for the government or in family business. As a result, Kuwait's labor legislation is largely a means of controlling foreign labor, although it has been applied to Kuwaitis in a number of cases.

This legislation provides for direct negotiations between employers and "laborers or their representatives" in the private sector. Most agreements are resolved in such negotiations; if not, either party may petition the Ministry of Social Affairs and Labor for mediation. If mediation fails, the dispute is referred to a labor arbitration board composed of officials from the High Court of Appeals, the Attorney General's office, and the Ministry of Social Affairs and Labor.

The law limits the right to strike. It requires all labor disputes to be referred to compulsory arbitration if labor and management cannot reach a solution. The law does not have any provision guaranteeing that strikers will be free from any legal or administrative action taken against them by the State. Two strikes occurred in 1994. One was called by cleaning personnel in the school system for a pay raise, and a second by security guards at the Social Welfare Home to collect unpaid wages. The majority of the strikers were foreign workers.

Kuwaiti law provides extensive protection for many classes of workers and Kuwait does have the best developed trade union system of any country in the Gulf. Workers can join trade unions, and over 28,400 people were organized in 14 unions in 1994, 12 of which are affiliated with the Kuwait Trade Union Federation (KTUF), the sole, legal trade union federation.

At the same time, the government maintains powerful internal security controls over union activity. It restricts the right of association by prohibiting all workers from freely establishing trade unions. The law stipulates that workers may establish only one union in any occupational trade, and that the unions may establish only one federation. The Bank Workers Union and the Kuwait Airways Workers Union are independent.

The Government has shown no sign that it would accept the establishment of more than one legal trade union federation. The law stipulates that any new union must include at least 100 workers, of whom at least 15 are citizens. This requirement discourages the establishment of unions in sectors employing few citizens, such as the construction industry and domestic servants.[197]

The government subsidizes as much as 90 percent of most union budgets. It can inspect the financial records of any union, and prohibit any union from engaging in vaguely defined political or religious activities. The courts can dissolve any union for violating labor laws or for threatening "public order and morals." The Emir may also dissolve a union by decree. By law, the Ministry of Social Affairs and Labor is authorized to seize the assets of any dissolved union. Although no union has been dissolved, the law subordinates the legal existence of unions to the power of the State.[198]

As is the case in all the Southern Gulf states, the treatment of foreign workers presents significant problems in terms of both internal security and human rights. Foreigners constitute most of Kuwait's total work force and more than one-third of its unionized work force. Yet the law discriminates against foreign workers by permitting them to join unions only after five years of residency and only as non-voting members.

Unlike union members who are citizens, foreign workers do not have the right to elect their leadership. The law requires that union officials

must be citizens. The ILO has criticized the five-year residency requirement and the denial of voting rights for foreign workers. KTUF adminis-
ters an Expatriate Labor Office which is authorized to investigate com-
plaints of foreign laborers and provide them with free legal advice. Any
foreign worker may submit a grievance to the Labor Office, regardless of
union status.[199]

The Constitution prohibits forced labor "except in cases specified by
law for national emergency and with just remuneration." Nonetheless,
there have been credible reports that foreign nationals employed as
domestic servants have been denied exit visas requested without their
employer's consent. Foreign workers may not change their employment
without permission from their original sponsors.

Domestic servants are particularly vulnerable to abuses, because they
are not protected by the Labor Law. In many cases employers exercise
some control over their servants by holding their passports, although the
Government prohibits this practice and has acted to retrieve passports of
maids involved in disputes. By law, domestic servants who run away
from their employers may be treated as criminals. In some reported cases,
employers illegally withheld wages from domestic servants to cover the
costs involved in bringing them to Kuwait. The State Department reports
that the government has done little, if anything, to protect domestics in
such cases.[200]

13

Strategic Interests

Kuwait faces serious strategic challenges. It must develop as effective a self-defense capability as is possible; it must reinforce its strategic ties to the US as the ultimate guarantor of its security; it must do as much as possible to reinforce its ties to other Southern Gulf states; and it must move towards political, social, and economic reform.

The Challenge of Self Defense

Kuwait is already doing a lot to improve its self-defense capabilities. It must, however, deal with three serious problems if these efforts are to be effective:

- First, Kuwait needs to make further reforms in the leadership of its armed forces, and firmly emphasize military professionalism even in the most senior positions. Kuwait, more than any other Southern Gulf state, faces urgent war fighting needs. These needs can only be met if promotion and rank are based on competence, rather than family. There needs to be a much clearer understanding within the highest echelons of the Kuwaiti government that the loyalty of modern armed forces is ultimately dependent on the belief by those in the armed forces that they have a clear mission, that this mission is being efficiently and honestly funded, and that their leadership is the best leadership available.
- Second, Kuwait needs to stop politicizing its arms purchases. It needs rigorous financial procedures, backed by active criminal prosecution, to ensure there is no corruption in such purchases. There is no doubt that the West—especially the US and Britain—have aggressively oversold arms systems, asked Kuwait for unfair "burden sharing" purchases, and contributed to a climate where some contracts have had dubious terms and kickbacks. Kuwait faces threats, however, which are too serious for such politics, and it needs

to demonstrate to its armed forces and its people that "business as usual" does not extend to defense.

- Most important, Kuwait as a whole needs to understand that nothing the government and royal family does can be a substitute for a public commitment to sharing in the burden of defense and providing the manpower Kuwait needs to make its forces effective. Kuwait cannot be defended by criticizing the government from within the security of a Diwania, or by hiring foreigners to substitute for its sons.

Kuwait has the capability to deal with these challenges, but neither Kuwait nor its allies should have any illusions about the results. Kuwait has no foreseeable prospect of being able to defend its own territory without external aid. It requires substantial additional arms deliveries if it is to create even a limited regional deterrent or to acquire the levels of munitions, weapons, and military facilities to allow either an Arab or US force to come to its aid. Without such arms imports, Kuwait will be hopelessly weak. Further, Kuwait's forces will remain dependent on foreign technicians and support during the next decade. It will be unable to use its arms against any nation without supplier assistance, although Iran and Iraq could operate many Kuwaiti weapons systems if these were seized in a future invasion.

The Challenge of Regional Cooperation

The Gulf Cooperation Council has set good goals, but its members have failed to support them. Regional cooperation offers no near or mid-term prospect of offering the kind of reinforcements that could defend Kuwait's northern border. The unfortunate fact is that the Southern Gulf states are failing to make practical progress in virtually every major area of collective defense. While individual states and the Gulf Cooperation Council have sometimes shown that they are capable of formulating the right plans and rhetoric, they have either not made sufficient progress or have failed to make any progress in many priority areas. The Southern Gulf states need to develop collective or integrated defense capabilities by:

- Creating an effective planning system for collective defense, and truly standardized and/or interoperable forces.
- Integrating C^{4}I and sensor nets for air and naval combat, including BVR and night warfare.
- Creating joint air defense and air attack capabilities.
- Establishing effective cross reinforcement and tactical mobility capabilities.

- Setting up joint training, support, and infrastructure facilities.
- Creating joint air and naval strike forces.
- Deploying joint land defenses of the Kuwaiti/Northwestern Saudi borders. Today's Peninsula Shield force is more farce than force. It has political value, but negligible warfighting capability against Iraqi armor.
- Preparing for outside or over-the-horizon reinforcement.
- Creating common advanced training systems.
- Improved urban and urban area security for unconventional warfare and low intensity combat.

They need to procure interoperable or standardized equipment to provide the capability to perform the following missions:

- Heavy armor, artillery, attack helicopters, and mobile air defense equipment for defense of the upper Gulf.
- Interoperability and standardization with US power projection forces.
- Interoperable offensive air capability with stand-off, all-weather precision weapons and anti-armor/anti-ship capability.
- Interoperable air defense equipment, including heavy surface-to-air missiles, BVR/AWX fighters, AEW & surveillance capability, ARM & ECM capability. (Growth to ATBM and cruise missile defense capability)
- Maritime surveillance systems, and equipment for defense against maritime surveillance, and unconventional warfare.
- Mine detection and clearing systems.
- Improved urban, area, and border security equipment for unconventional warfare and low intensity conflict.
- Advanced training aids.
- Support and sustainment equipment.

Kuwait and its GCC partners also need to develop coordinated procurement plans to eliminate the waste of defense on:

- Unique equipment types and one-of-a-kind modifications.
- "Glitter factor" weapons; "developmental" equipment and technology.
- Non-interoperable weapons and systems.
- Submarines and ASW systems.
- Major surface warfare ships.
- Major equipment for divided or "dual" forces.
- New types of equipment which increase the maintenance, sustainability, and training problem, or layer new types over old.

While outside Arab forces could help secure Kuwait, Egypt is the only Arab nation that has the potential strength to provide Kuwait with the kind of sustainable and combat effective forces needed to deal with Iraq, and Egyptian forces are not structured to provide this kind of power projection force. Even if Kuwait and Egypt reached a political and financial agreement, Egypt lacks anything approaching the high technology power projection capabilities of the United States.

At the same time, every improvement in regional cooperation will be important, particularly within the Gulf and between Kuwait, Saudi Arabia, and Bahrain. Kuwait and Saudi Arabia need to coordinate tightly on land defense. At the same time, Kuwait, Saudi Arabia, and Bahrain need to integrate their air and missile defenses, air strike-attack capabilities, and maritime surveillance, mine warfare, and surface defense capabilities. All three states need to recognize that the GCC is not enough, that the Peninsular Shield Force will only be as strong as its Kuwait-Saudi component, and that it is the mutual cooperation among Bahrain, Kuwait, and Saudi Arabia which will shape the most important elements of their deterrent and defense capabilities, and ability to support reinforcements from the West.

The Challenge of Relations
with the United States and the West

Kuwait will require the support of US and other Western forces in any serious crisis with Iraq and Iran until well after the year 2010. Kuwait understood this when it signed a 10 year joint defense agreement with the US on September 19, 1991. This agreement allowed the US to preposition stocks and equipment on Kuwaiti soil and to deploy a squadron of combat aircraft in Kuwait, while giving the US access to its ports and airfields in an emergency.

The agreement required Kuwait to pay the US $215 million for prepositioning aid and support, including $50 million in 1992. Prepositioning was to include the equipment for three armored companies and three mechanized companies, including 58 M-1A2 tanks, M-2s, artillery, and other equipment, plus the construction of some $125 million in storage and reception facilities. A new US Army storage area is being constructed some 40 kilometers south of Kuwait City.[201]

The agreement also provided for joint training. Kuwaiti and US forces completed two joint exercises by May, 1992. One involved 2,300 Marines and the other 1,000 special forces. It has continued regular joint exercise training ever since. The US also held its first joint military command exercise with military commanders from the GCC states in Kuwait in December, 1994. Other series of exercises include Iris Gold, Eager, Eager Archer,

Homeland Shield, Intrinsic Action, and Native Fury. Many of these series involve Britain and France, as well as Kuwait and the US.[202]

The need for strategic cooperation between the Kuwait and the US became all too clear in August and September of 1992. The confrontation between Iraq and the UN over the elimination of weapons of mass destruction, and Iraq's treatment of its Shi'ites and Kurds, forced the US to transform US Army, Marine Corps, and Navy exercises into a demonstration that the US would protect Kuwait against any military adventures by Iraq. The US had to rush Patriot batteries to both Kuwait and Bahrain. It also conducted a test pre-positioning exercise called Native Fury 92, deployed a 1,300 man battalion from the 1st Cavalry Division, and conducted an amphibious reinforcement exercise called Eager Mace 92. It deployed 1,900 Marines and 2,400 soldiers, including two armored and two mechanized companies.[203]

This need for joint exercises became even more apparent in October, 1994, when Iraq moved its Hammurabi and Al Nida Republican Guards divisions south from the area around Baghdad to positions about 20 kilometers from the border with Kuwait. Although Iraq backed down, and agreed to withdraw its forces on October 9, 1994, this crisis made it clear that the military balance in the Gulf is shaped by a combination of US and Kuwaiti actions and not by the GCC or unified action by the GCC.

The October, 1994 crisis again exposed the fact that Kuwait had virtually no strategic depth, and that both Iraq and Iran could rapidly threaten Kuwait in a crisis. It demonstrated Kuwait's inability to act alone, and that the Gulf states must do everything possible to reduce the problems the US faced in deploying its forces, even with prepositioning.

While the US was better prepared on this occasion for rapid movement than in 1990, it took 72 to 96 hours for the first combat aircraft to arrive. The closest US prepositioning ships were six days sailing away in Diego Garcia, and it took well over a week for US Army forces in the US to move by air, fully deploy to their prepositioned equipment in Kuwait, and move to the border area in combat sustainable form. While US power projection capabilities for mid-to-high intensity warfare were not tested during this confrontation with Iraq, the US Army later issued briefings that indicated that even with all the force improvements the US had programmed for 1998, it would still take 30 days to fully deploy two sustainable heavy divisions and one light division, and 75 days to deploy the kind of five division corps called for in its Major Regional Contingency strategy.[204]

Further, Kuwait and the US were confronted by new indications of Iraqi movements against Kuwait in August and September, 1995. These indications led Kuwait to create a new security zone near its capital, and the US to rush naval reinforcements and maritime prepositioning ships to the Gulf. The US deployed a total of 12 prepositioning ships from Diego Garcia and other locations to the Gulf, with enough armor, artillery, food, fuel, water, vehicles, and other equipment to sustain a 16,500 Marine Corps MEF (Forward), and a 15,000–17,000 man US Army force in combat.[205] They also led Kuwait and the US to advance the date of a large amphibious exercise called Eager Mace 96-1 to deter any Iraqi moves.[206]

The US and Kuwait cooperated again in January, 1996, when US intelligence concluded that Iraq had brought five armored divisions to sufficient readiness to deploy to Kuwait with only five hours notice. The US deployed 12 prepositioning ships—enough to equip a Marine Division and a US Army Brigade—into the Gulf. The US did not send troops, but this move allowed the US to deploy up to 20,000 troops on short notice. The US also deployed additional combat aircraft to Bahrain and Kuwait, and extended a joint exercise with Kuwait.

The US already had some 20,000 troops in the Middle East area, and deployed 35 ships, and 14,000 sailors and US Marines, in its Fifth Fleet between the Suez Canal and Indian Ocean. These forces included the *Nimitz* carrier battle group, and a Marine Corps amphibious ready group. It is interesting to note that the US only had 250 naval personnel stationed permanently ashore in Bahrain.[207]

It is clear, therefore, that Kuwaiti strategic cooperation with the US will be critical in the years to come, as will efforts to provide adequate power projection and rapid response capabilities. Kuwait and the US have already demonstrated that they can work well together, but this cooperation can only be successful if the other Southern Gulf states provide equal support, particularly in improving US prepositioning and rapid deployment capabilities.

Although less urgent, Kuwait must also expand its strategic relations with other countries. This is a challenge that Kuwait has done a good job of meeting. It has signed four defense agreements with the UK since 1991. It signed one 10 year pact with the UK on March 11, 1992, which covers technical and training assistance and bilateral exercises and trilateral exercises between Kuwait, the UK, and the US. These exercises have already included Blue Falcon, Free Sky, Eager Mace, and Eager Sentry. It signed another agreement on August 31, 1992 for technical cooperation, and an arms sales protocol on September 22, 1992. It reached a contracting agreement on December 2, 1992.[208]

Kuwait reached its first defense agreement with France in 1969, and made several major purchases of French arms in the 1970s and 1980s. It signed two new agreements after the Gulf War on August 18, 1992, and October 18, 1993. The first agreement provided for technical assistance, modernization of the Kuwaiti Navy, and joint maneuvers like Gulf Pearl and Pearl of the West. The second agreement established new legal conditions for arms sales. Kuwait holds regular land and naval exercises with France, and began joint air exercises with France in June, 1994.[209]

Kuwait established diplomatic relations with Russia in 1963, and signed arms sales contracts with Russia in 1975 and 1982. It signed an agreement with Russia on February 16, 1993, covering the exchange of military delegations and information, and a cooperation agreement on arms sales and joint exercises on November 29, 1993. Kuwait has since carried out Exercise Rikka with Russia, and signed a major arms sales contract on August 8, 1994. Kuwait signed an agreement with China on March 24, 1995, under which China will provide Kuwait with aid to reorganize its armed forces. It has also held three joint exercises with the Italian Navy since 1991.[210]

Kuwait's security ties to the West are critical to Kuwait's future security. They do, however, present problems that both Kuwait and its allies must deal with in the future:

- The first problem is that such ties create the risk that Kuwait will become so dependent on states outside the region that it will not properly develop its own defense capabilities, will become over-reliant on outside support for low-level security contingencies that require a constant Kuwaiti effort and immediate reaction, and will fail to assert its own sovereignty. Some of the National Assembly debates over defense are a warning that this may already be happening.
- The second is that dependence on the West will lead Kuwait to under-emphasize the importance of collective security with Bahrain and Saudi Arabia, and the need to at least try to expand the capabilities of the Gulf Cooperation Council. So far, Kuwait has sought to expand its collective security efforts, but it almost certainly needs to do more.
- The third is that ties to so many countries will encourage buying arms from every possible source and politicizing arms purchases at the expense of standardization, interoperability, effectiveness, and waste. The previous discussion of Kuwait's arms purchases provides a number of indications that this is becoming a serious problem.
- The fourth is that Kuwait's growing dependence on the US will lead the US to abuse its burden-sharing negotiations with Kuwait, and to seek more support than is really merited. There are strong indications that the US is already abusing its burden-sharing negotiations and is asking for payments for very dubious charges, such as "depreciation" on the carrier battle groups it has deployed to the Gulf.

There is no reason Kuwait cannot deal with these problems if both its leadership and the National Assembly are willing to accept their importance. Kuwait's leadership already seems to understand what needs to be done. The question is whether its National Assembly can look beyond the role of critic and focus on the nation's strategic priorities.

The Challenge of Internal Reform

No nation can be secure, or meet its strategic needs, without meeting the needs of its own people. Kuwait has done well in adapting to the challenges of reconstruction, and its economy is recovering, but Kuwait faces the same need to make internal reforms as the other Southern Gulf states. Kuwait must develop its own answer to the problem of increasing popular participation in political decision-making. Kuwait must redefine its citizenship to include many of its Bidoon and long-term "foreign" residents. It must simultaneously reduce its dependence on foreign labor, create more jobs for Kuwaitis, and privatize much of its economy. It must adopt fiscal reforms and replace an unaffordable welfare state with a new mix of social services and a much larger and more competitive private sector.

This is not to argue that Kuwait must copy Western social, economic, and political practices. In fact, all of these reforms have been advocated by many Kuwaitis and are already the subject of public debate in Kuwait. The problem in the Gulf, however, is rarely expertise and intelligence, it is rather the need for commitment and action. It is also the understanding on the part of its intellectuals, politically active citizens, and technocrats that "reform" involves far more than simply criticizing the nation's leaders or seeking added political power. Kuwait's small population and wealth give it more time in which to carry out such internal reforms than is available to many of its neighbors. Even so, this time is measured in years and not in decades.

As has been discussed earlier, these reforms should include efforts to:

- Reduce dependence on welfare, and reserve subsidies only for its poor citizens. Water, electricity, motor gasoline, basic foods, and many services need to be priced at market levels and subsidies to citizens need to be replaced with jobs and economic opportunities.
- Force radical reductions in the number of foreign workers, with priority for reductions in servants and in trades that allow the most rapid conversion to native labor. Charge high fees for foreign labor permits and force all foreign labor to pay not only the cost of all government services, but pay a premium over cost.
- Force social changes in Kuwait by eliminating guaranteed employment in the government and ensuring that government salaries lag sharply behind those in the private sector. Kuwait's young and well-

educated population needs to be given jobs, and Kuwaiti society must adapt to the reality that its present dependence on foreign labor is a major threat to Kuwait's national identity and security.

- Educate Kuwaitis to regard government jobs as having low status and to understand that most government jobs are now a net liability to the Kuwaiti economy. Freeze and then reduce the number of civil servants. Restructure and down-size the civil service to focus on productive areas of activity with a much smaller pool of manpower. Cut back sharply on state employees by the year 2000.

- Restructure the educational system to focus on job training and competitiveness. Create strong new incentives for faculty and students to focus on job-related education, sharply down-size other forms of educational funding and activity, and eliminate high overhead educational activities without economic benefits.

- Eliminate economic disincentives for employers hiring native labor, and create disincentives for hiring foreign labor.

- Shift all government impacted goods and services to market prices. Remove distortions in the economy and underpricing of water, oil, and gas.

- Implement extensive privatization to increase the efficiency of Kuwaiti investments in downstream and upstream operations. Create real jobs and career opportunities for native Kuwaitis, and open investment opportunities up to a much wider range of investors. Kuwait has already begun this process but it needs to be sharply accelerated to remove productive activity from government control. At the same time, privatization must be managed in ways that ensure all Kuwaitis an opportunity to share in the privatization process. It should not be conducted in a way that benefits only a small elite group of investors and discourages popular confidence and willingness to invest in Kuwait.

- Stop subsidizing Kuwaiti businesses in ways which prevent realistic economic growth and development, and which deprive the government of revenue. Present policies strongly favor Kuwaiti citizens and Kuwaiti-owned companies. Income taxes are only levied on foreign corporations and foreign interests in Kuwaiti corporations, at rates that may range as high as 55 percent of net income.

- Tax earnings and sales with progressive taxes that reduce or eliminate budget deficits, encourage local investment, and create strong disincentives for the expatriation of capital, including all foreign holdings of capital and property by members of elite and ruling families. This will provide a key source of revenue, and make the distribution of income more equitable. Kuwait needs to ensure that wealthier Kuwaiti's make a proper contribution to social services and defense.

- Allow foreign investment on more competitive terms. Kuwait currently allows foreign investment in limited sectors of the economy, in minority partnerships, and on terms compatible with continued Kuwaiti control of all basic economic activities. Some sectors of the economy—including oil, banking, insurance and real estate—have traditionally been closed to foreign investment. Foreigners (with the exception of nationals from some GCC states) are not permitted to trade in Kuwaiti stocks on the Kuwaiti Stock Exchange, except through the medium of unit trusts. Protection should not, however, extend to the point where it eliminates efficiency and competitiveness, or restricts economic expansion. Foreign nationals, who represent a majority of the population, are prohibited from having majority ownership in virtually every business other than certain small service-oriented businesses and may not own property (there are some exceptions for citizens of other GCC states). Kuwait needs to act on proposals such as allowing foreign equity participation in the banking sector (up to 40 percent) and in the upstream oil sector (terms still to be determined).
- Reform the structure of the budget to ensure that most of the nation's revenues and foreign reserves and earnings are integrated into the national budget and into the planning process. Clearly separate royal and national income and investment holdings.
- Place sharp limits on the transfer of state funds to princes and members of the royal family outside the actual ruling family, and transfers of unearned income to members of other leading families. Ensure that such family members are fully taxed on all income and investments.
- Ensure that all income from enterprises with state financing is reflected in the national budget and is integrated into the national economic development and planning program.
- Establish ruthlessly demanding market criteria for evaluating and making all major state and state-supported investments. Require state investments to offer a conclusively higher rate of return than private investments. Demand detailed and independent risk assessment and projections of comparative return on investment, with a substantial penalty for state versus privately funded projects and ventures. Down-size the scale of programs to reduce investment and cash flow costs and the risk of cost-escalation.
- Create new incentives to invest in local industries and business and disincentives for the expatriation of capital.
- Create market driven incentives for foreign investment in major oil and gas projects, refineries, and petrochemical operations. Avoid offset requirements that simply create disguised unemployment or

non-competitive ventures that act as a further state-sponsored distortion of the economy.

- Establish a firm rule of law for all property, contract, permitting, and business activity and reduce state bureaucratic and permitting barriers to private investment.
- Place national security spending on the same basis as other state spending, and fully implement the law the National Assembly passed in 1993 to insure that all direct and indirect defense costs—including arms—are reflected in the national budget. Integrate it fully into the national budget, including investment and equipment purchases.
- Replace the present emphasis on judging arms purchases of the basis on initial procurement costs and technical features with a full assessment of life cycle cost—including training, maintenance, and facilities.
- Cease buying arms in an effort to win outside political support and establish specific procedures and regulations for evaluating the value of standardization and interoperability with existing national equipment and facilities, those of other Gulf states, and those of the US and other power projection forces.
- Subject all offset proposals relating to government military and non-military expenditures abroad to the same risk and cost-benefit analyses used by the private sector, and create independent auditing procedures to ensure that offsets do not become a concealed government subsidy or a way of benefiting influential government officials.
- Expand the number of voters for the National Assembly. Continue to allow the expansion of political activity to ensure the peaceful resolution of internal economic debates.
- Deal with the issue of the Bidoon and expand citizenship to de facto Kuwaitis.
- Create a long-term planning effort focusing on periods five, ten, and twenty years into the future to set goals for Kuwait's social, economic, and military development, with special attention to the problems of population growth, reducing dependence on foreign labor, diversifying the economy, and linking development to a clear set of social goals. Use contingency and risk analysis, not simply growth-oriented models.

Notes

Chapter 1

1. *Oil and Gas Journal*, September 23, 1991, p. 62; 6; and IEA, *Middle East Oil and Gas*, Paris, OECD/IEA, 1995, Annexes 1C and 2I.

2. The military manpower, force strength, and equipment estimates in this section are made by the author using a wide range of sources, including computerized data bases, interviews, and press clipping services. Most are impossible to reference in ways of use to the reader. The force strength statistics are generally taken from interviews, and from the sources reference for each paragraph. The data for the pre–Gulf War estimates also draw heavily on his *The Gulf and the Search for Strategic Stability* (Boulder, Westview, 1984) and *The Gulf and the West* (Boulder, Westview, 1988).

Extensive use has also been made of the annual editions of the International Institute for Strategic Studies *Military Balance* (IISS, London), in this case, the 1995–1996 edition, and of the Jaffee Center for Strategic Studies, *The Military Balance in the Middle East* (JCSS, Tel Aviv), especially the 1994–1995 edition and working materials from the coming edition. Material has also been drawn from computer print outs from NEXIS, the United States Naval Institute data base, and from the DMS/FI Market Intelligence Reports data base. Other sources include *Jane's Defense Weekly*, December 14, 1991, p. 1174, March 28, 1992, pp. 528–531; *New York Times*, January 14, 1992, p. 4; *London Financial Times*, July 8, 1991, p. 3, January 7, 1992, p. 4; *Defense News*, February 10, 1992, p. 38; Theodore Craig, "Kuwait: Background, Restoration, and Questions for the United States," Congressional Research Service, 91-288F, May 21, 1992; Department of Defense, *Conduct of the Persian Gulf War; Final Report to Congress*, Washington, Department of Defense, April, 1992, pp. 2–10; *Military Technology* "World Defense Almanac for 1991–1992," published in early 1992; Foreign Affairs Division, "Middle East Arms Control and Related Issues," Washington, Congressional Research Service, 91-384F, May 1, 1991; and *Middle East Economic Digest*, "Special Report: Defense," Volume 35, December 13, 1991.

Weapons data are taken from many sources, including computerized material available in NEXIS, and various editions of *Jane's Fighting Ships* (Jane's Publishing); *Jane's Naval Weapons Systems* (Jane's Publishing); *Jane's Armor and Artillery* (Jane's Publishing); *Jane's Infantry Weapons* (Jane's Publishing); *Jane's Military Vehicles and Logistics* (Jane's Publishing); *Jane's Land-Base Air Defense* (Jane's Publishing); *Jane's All the World's Aircraft* (Jane's Publishing); *Jane's Battlefield Surveillance Systems*, (Jane's Publishing); *Jane's Radar and Electronic Warfare Systems* (Jane's Publishing), *Jane's C3I Systems* (Jane's Publishing); *Jane's Air-Launched Weapons Systems* (Jane's

Publishing); *Jane's Defense Appointments & Procurement Handbook (Middle East Edition)* (Jane's Publishing); *Tanks of the World* (Bernard and Grafe); *Weyer's Warships* (Bernard and Grafe); and *Warplanes of the World* (Bernard and Grafe).

Other military background, effectiveness, strength, organizational, and history data are taken from Anthony H. Cordesman, *The Gulf and the Search for Strategic Stability*, Boulder, Westview, 1984, *The Gulf and the West*, Boulder, Westview, 1988, and *Weapons of Mass Destruction in the Middle East*, London, Brassey's/RUSI, 1991; Anthony H. Cordesman and Abraham Wagner, *The Lessons of Modern War, Volume II*, Boulder, Westview, 1989; the relevant country or war sections of Herbert K. Tillema, *International Conflict Since 1945*, Boulder, Westview, 1991; Department of Defense and Department of State, *Congressional Presentation for Security Assistance Programs, Fiscal Year 1993*, Washington, Department of State, 1992; various annual editions of John Laffin's *The World in Conflict* or *War Annual*, London, Brassey's, and John Keegan, *World Armies*, London, Macmillan, 1983.

3. The ranges shown cover the low and high case. The source of these projections is EIA, Oil Market Simulation Model Spreadsheet, 1994, data provided by the EIA Energy Markets and Contingency Information Division, and EIA, *International Energy Outlook, 1994*, pp. 11–20.

4. For further details on the strategic history of Kuwait, see Helen Chapin Meter, *Persian Gulf States*, Washington, Department of the Army DA Pam 550-185, 1993, and Anthony H. Cordesman, *The Gulf and the West*, Boulder, Westview, 1994.

Chapter 2

5. Alfred B. Prados, "Iraq and Kuwait: Conflicting Historical Claims," Congressional Research Service, 91-34F, January 11, 1991, p. 4.

6. *American Arab Affairs*, Fall 1989, p. 30; *Los Angeles Times*, December 2, 1990, pp. M-4 and M-8; Theodore Craig, "Kuwait: Background, Restoration, and Questions for the United States," Congressional Research Service, 91-288F, May 21, 1992, p. 9.

7. *Washington Post*, December 19, 1987, p. A-27.

8. Department of Defense, *Conduct of the Persian Gulf War; Final Report to Congress*, Washington, Department of Defense, April, 1992, pp. 6–7.

9. Department of Defense, *Conduct of the Persian Gulf War; Final Report to Congress*, Washington, Department of Defense, April, 1992, pp. 3–4.

10. Department of Defense, *Conduct of the Persian Gulf War; Final Report to Congress*, Washington, Department of Defense, April, 1992, pp. 3–4.

11. Alfred B. Prados, "Iraq and Kuwait: Conflicting Historical Claims," Congressional Research Service, 91-34F, January 11, 1991, p. 4.

12. FBIS NES-90-138, July 18, 1990, p. 21; Theodore Craig, "Kuwait: Background, Restoration, and Questions for the United States," Congressional Research Service, 91-288F, May 21, 1992, p. 8; Department of Defense, *Conduct of the Persian Gulf War; Final Report to Congress*, Washington, Department of Defense, April, 1992, pp. 2–10.

13. *Jane's Defense Weekly*, February 22, 1992, p. 274, March 7, 1992, p. 375, August 1, 1992, p. A-10, August 4, 1992, p. A-14, August 8, 1992, p. 6, August

15, 1992, p. A-15; *Defense News*, September 9, 1991, p. 1, November 18, 1991, p. 3, February 17, 1992, p. 3, June 15, 1992, p. 26; *Stars and Stripes*, March 3, 1992, p. 8; *London Financial Times*, July 8, 1991, p. 3; *Washington Post*, August 28, 1991, p. A-7, September 6, 1991, p. A-24, August 15, 1992, p. A-15; *Washington Times*, December 6, 1991, p. A-2, August 5, 1992, p. A-1; *Aviation Week*, September 9, 1991, p. 21.

14. The border was laid out relatively quickly by a single British agent, Major John More, and no follow-up effort was made to create a formal survey or border markings. *Economist*, February 29, 1992m p. 45; *Philadelphia Inquirer*, February 20, 1992, p. A-16; *Wall Street Journal*, December 5, 1991, p. A-1.

15. Department of Defense background briefing, October 20, 1994 (Federal News Service); Department of Defense handouts of October 11, 1994 and October 12, 1994; *Jane's Defense Weekly*, October 22, 1994, p. 4, December 17, 1994, p. 7; US Army briefing sheet (undated) October, 1994; Congressional Research Service, *Iraq Crisis, October, 1994, A Chronology*, 94-808F, October 24, 1994.

16. This description is based on interviews with US experts, and Executive News Service, August 29, 1995, 0329, September 19, 1995, 1014, September 27, 1995, 0324; Washington Post, August 19, 1995, p. A-17.

17. *Baltimore Sun*, December 29, 1995, p. 16A; *Defense News*, April 18, 1995, p. 10; *Wall Street Journal*, June 27, 1995, p. A-10.

18. *Defense News*, April 18, 1995, p. 10; *Wall Street Journal*, June 27, 1995, p. A-10.

19. Executive News Service, October 10, 1995, 0221.

20. CIA, *World Factbook, 1995*, "Kuwait"; *Jane's Defense Weekly*, July 29, 1995, p. 15.

Chapter 3

21. "Special Report Kuwait," *Middle East Economic Digest*, February 23, 1996, p. 7.

22. Estimates based upon the data in "Special Report Kuwait," *Middle East Economic Digest*, February 23, 1996, p. 15; ACDA, World Military Expenditures and Arms Transfers, 1993–1994, Table I, and CIA, *World Factbook, 1995*, and Yousef H. Al-Ebraheem, "The Gulf Economic Situation in the Next Decade: The Case of Kuwait," National Defense University Workshop on Gulf Security, April, 1996, p. 10. Further statistical and analytic background is taken from material provided by the World Bank, including "Will Arab Workers Prosper or Be Left Out in the Twenty-First Century?," August, 1995; "Forging a Partnership for Environmental Action," December, 1994; and "A Population Perspective on Development: The Middle East and North Africa," August, 1994.

23. World Bank, "Forging a Partnership for Environmental Action," December, 1994; and "A Population Perspective on Development: The Middle East and North Africa," Washington, World Bank, August, 1994, p. 24.

24. CIA, *World Factbook, 1995*, UAE.

25. Energy Information Agency (EIA), *International Energy Outlook, 1994*, DOE/EIA 0484(94), July, 1994, pp. 14–26; EIA, *International Petroleum Status Report*, DOE/EIA 0520(94)1), November, 1994, pp. 6–7, and *International Petroleum Encyclopedia*, 1993, p. 280. These estimates have become increasingly more politi-

cal in recent years as each major producer in the Gulf has tried to exaggerate its reserves and relative importance.

26. IEA, *Middle East Oil and Gas*, Paris, OECD/IEA, 1995, p. 158.

27. "Special Report Kuwait," *Middle East Economic Digest*, February 24, 1995, pp. 12–16.

28. This discussion of Kuwaiti energy developments is adapted from material provided in the DOE/EIA Internet data base, EIA, analysis section, country chapters, as accessed on July 15, 1995 and March 9, 1996; and IEA, *Middle East Oil and Gas*, Paris, OECD/IEA, 1995.

29. *Oil and Gas Journal*, September 23, 1991, p. 62.

30. IEA, *Middle East Oil and Gas*, Paris, OECD/IEA, 1995, pp. 153–157.

31. IEA, *Middle East Oil and Gas*, Paris, OECD/IEA, 1995, pp. 153–157.

32. IEA, *Middle East Oil and Gas*, Paris, OECD/IEA, 1995, pp. 155–160.

33. Energy Information Agency (EIA), *International Energy Outlook, 1994*, DOE/EIA 0484(94), July, 1994, pp. 14–26; EIA, *International Petroleum Status Report*, DOE/EIA 0520(94)1), November, 1994, pp. 6–7, and *International Petroleum Encyclopedia*, 1993, p. 280. These estimates have become increasingly more political in recent years as each major producer in the Gulf has tried to exaggerates its reserves and relative importance.

34. This discussion of Kuwait energy developments is adapted from material provided in the DOE/EIA Internet data base, EIA, analysis section, country chapters, as accessed on July 15, 1995 and March 9, 1996; and IEA, *Middle East Oil and Gas*, Paris, OECD/IEA, 1995.

35. This discussion of Kuwait energy developments is adapted from material provided in the DOE/EIA Internet data base, EIA, analysis section, country chapters, as accessed on July 15, 1995 and March 9, 1996; and IEA, *Middle East Oil and Gas*, Paris, OECD/IEA, 1995.

36. "Special Report Kuwait," *Middle East Economic Digest*, February 24, 1995, pp. 12–16.

37. This discussion of Kuwait energy developments is adapted from material provided in the DOE/EIA Internet data base, EIA, analysis section, country chapters, as accessed on July 15, 1995 and March 9, 1996; and IEA, *Middle East Oil and Gas*, Paris, OECD/IEA, 1995.

38. *Middle East Economic Digest*, February 24, 1995, p. 14.

39. *Wall Street Journal*, June 27, 1995, p. A-10.

40. This discussion of Kuwait energy developments is adapted from material provided in the DOE/EIA Internet data base, EIA, analysis section, country chapters, as accessed on July 15, 1995 and March 9, 1996; and IEA, *Middle East Oil and Gas*, Paris, OECD/IEA, 1995.

41. This discussion of Kuwait energy developments is adapted from material provided in the DOE/EIA Internet data base, EIA, analysis section, country chapters, as accessed on July 15, 1995 and March 9, 1996; and IEA, *Middle East Oil and Gas*, Paris, OECD/IEA, 1995.

42. "Special Report Kuwait," *Middle East Economic Digest*, February 24, 1995, pp. 12–16.

43. This discussion of Kuwait energy developments is adapted from material provided in the DOE/EIA Internet data base, EIA, analysis section, country chapters, as accessed on July 15, 1995 and March 9, 1996; and IEA, Middle East Oil and Gas, Paris, OECD/IEA, 1995.

44. "Special Report Kuwait," *Middle East Economic Digest*, February 23, 1996, p. 15; *New York Times*, July 17, 1995, p. D-4.

45. This discussion of Kuwait energy developments is adapted from material provided in the DOE/EIA Internet data base, EIA, analysis section, country chapters, as accessed on July 15, 1995 and March 9, 1996; and IEA, *Middle East Oil and Gas*, Paris, OECD/IEA, 1995, Annexes 1C and 2I.

46. This discussion of Kuwait energy developments is adapted from material provided in the DOE/EIA Internet data base, EIA, analysis section, country chapters, as accessed on July 15, 1995 and March 9, 1996; and IEA, *Middle East Oil and Gas*, Paris, OECD/IEA, 1995, Annexes 1C and 2I.

47. *Middle East Economic Digest*, February 23, 1996, p. 14.

48. EIA, *Monthly Energy Review*, August, 1995, p. 130; "Special Report Kuwait," *Middle East Economic Digest*, February 24, 1995, pp. 9–22; CIA, *World Factbook, 1994*, pp. 220–221.

49. "Special Report Kuwait," *Middle East Economic Digest*, February 24, 1995, pp. 9–22; CIA, *World Factbook, 1994*, pp. 220–221; *Wall Street Journal*, June 4, 1996, p. A-14.

50. *Wall Street Journal*, June 4, 1996, p. A-14.

51. This discussion of Kuwait energy developments is adapted from material provided in the DOE/EIA Internet data base, EIA, analysis section, country chapters, as accessed on July 15, 1995 and March 9, 1996; and IEA, *Middle East Oil and Gas*, Paris, OECD/IEA, 1995, Annexes 1C and 2I.

52. Yousef H. Al-Ebraheem, "The Gulf Economic Situation in the Next Decade: The Case of Kuwait," National Defense University Workshop on Gulf Security, April, 1996, p. 10.

53. It is typical of the serious conflicts in data on the Gulf that there are very different figures in other Ministry of Finance documents. Another estimate of the public budget in millions of Kuwaiti Dinars is as follows:

	Revenues	*Expenditures*	*Surplus/Deficit*
1989/1990	3,234.6	3,095.7	138.9
1990/1991	273	7,613.9	−7,390.7
1991/1992	647.3	6,111.5	−5,464.2
1992/1993	2,363.7	3,936.3	−1,572.6
1993/1994	2,775.1	4,240.8	−1,465.7
1994/1995	3,100.7	4,193.2	−1,092.5
1995/1996	2,910	4,230	−1,320.0

54. "Special Report Kuwait," *Middle East Economic Digest*, February 24, 1995, pp. 9–22; CIA, *World Factbook, 1995*, "Kuwait."

55. Armed Force Journal, August, 1995, p. 22;

56. *"Jane's Defense Weekly,* July 29, 1995, pp. 17–36; "Special Report Kuwait," *Middle East Economic Digest,* February 24, 1995, pp. 9–22; Special Report Kuwait," February 24, 1995, pp. 9–22; June 16, 1995; June 23, 1995, July 21, 1995, p. 11, August 11, 1995, pp. 10–11, August 25, 1995, p. 23, September 1, 1995, pp. 6–7.

57. *Middle East Economic Digest,* July 21, 1995, p. 11; *Jane's Defense Weekly,* July 29, 1995, pp. 17–36; "Special Report Kuwait," *Middle East Economic Digest,* February 24, 1995, pp. 9–22.

58. Yousef H. Al-Ebraheem, "The Gulf Economic Situation in the Next Decade: The Case of Kuwait," National Defense University Workshop on Gulf Security, April, 1996, p. 12.

59. US State Department, Internet data base, economic report on Kuwait, accessed June 20, 1995; *Middle East Economic Digest,* July 21, 1995, p. 11; *Jane's Defense Weekly,* July 29, 1995, pp. 17–36.

60. US State Department, Internet data base, economic report on Kuwait, accessed June 20, 1995; *Middle East Economic Digest,* July 21, 1995, p. 11; *Jane's Defense Weekly,* July 29, 1995, pp. 17–36.

61. "Special Report Kuwait," *Middle East Economic Digest,* February 23, 1996, p. 8; *Middle East Economic Digest,* July 21, 1995, p. 11; "Special Report Kuwait," *Middle East Economic Digest,* February 24, 1995, pp. 9–22; "Special Report Kuwait," *Middle East Economic Digest,* February 24, 1995, pp. 9–22; CIA, *World Factbook, 1994,* pp. 220–221; *Middle East Economic Digest,* June 16, 1995, August 25, 1995, p. 23, September 1, 1995, p. 6.

62. EIA, *Monthly Energy Review,* August, 1995, p. 130; "Special Report Kuwait," *Middle East Economic Digest,* February 24, 1995, pp. 9–22; CIA, *World Factbook, 1994,* pp. 220–221.

63. *Middle East Economic Digest,* July 21, 1995, p. 11; *Jane's Defense Weekly,* July 29, 1995, pp. 17–36; "Special Report Kuwait," *Middle East Economic Digest,* February 24, 1995, pp. 9–22; CIA, *World Factbook, 1994,* pp. 220–221.

64. World Bank, *World Population Projections, 1994–1995,* Washington, World Bank, 1994; *Middle East Economic Digest,* July 28, 1995, p. 11, February 23, 1996, p. 10; *CIA World Factbook,* 1995, "Iran."

65. CIA, *World Factbook, 1994,* pp. 220–221; *Middle East Economic Digest,* July 21, 1995, p. 11; *Jane's Defense Weekly,* July 29, 1995, pp. 17–36; *Jane's Defense Weekly,* July 29, 1995, p. 18.

66. Economist Intelligence Unit, *Country Profile: Kuwait,* London, 1996, pp. 13–14; Yousef H. Al-Ebraheem, "The Gulf Economic Situation in the Next Decade: The Case of Kuwait," National Defense University Workshop on Gulf Security, April, 1996, p. 12.

67. CIA, *World Factbook, 1995;* Economist Intelligence Unit, *Country Profile: Kuwait,* London, 1996, pp. 13–14. Further statistical and analytic background is taken from material provided by the World Bank, including "Will Arab Workers Prosper or Be Left Out in the Twenty-First Century?" August, 1995; "Forging a Partnership for Environmental Action," December, 1994; and "A Population Perspective on Development: The Middle East and North Africa," August, 1994.

68. Economist Intelligence Unit, *Country Profile: Kuwait*, London, 1996, p. 10.

69. Economist Intelligence Unit, *Country Profile: Kuwait*, London, 1996, pp. 10–14; CIA, *World Factbook, 1995;* Economist Intelligence Unit, *Country Profile: Kuwait*, London, 1996, pp. 13–14. Further statistical and analytic background is taken from material provided by the World Bank, including "Will Arab Workers Prosper or Be Left Out in the Twenty-First Century?" August, 1995; "Forging a Partnership for Environmental Action," December, 1994; and "A Population Perspective on Development: The Middle East and North Africa," August, 1994.

70. See Peter Carlson, "Castles in the Sand," *Washington Post Magazine*, January 14, 1996; Mary Tetrault, "Gulf Winds," *Current History*, 1996; F. Gregory Gause, *Oil Monarchies: Domestic and Security Challenges in the Arab Gulf States*, New York, Council on Foreign Relations, 1994.

71. CIA, *World Factbook, 1995*. Further statistical and analytic background is taken from material provided by the World Bank, including "Will Arab Workers Prosper or Be Left Out in the Twenty-First Century?" August, 1995; "Forging a Partnership for Environmental Action," December, 1994; and "A Population Perspective on Development: The Middle East and North Africa," August, 1994.

72. *Middle East Economic Digest*, February 24, 1995, pp. 9–22; Special Report Kuwait," February 24, 1995, pp. 9–22; June 16, 1995, p. 8; June 23, 1995, July 21, 1995, p. 11, August 11, 1995, pp. 10–11, August 25, 1995, p. 23, September 1, 1995, pp. 6–7; *Los Angeles Times*, June 27, 1995, p. C-3.

73. *New York Times*, July 17, 1995, p. D-4; *Wall Street Journal*, June 27, 1995, p. A-10.

74. CIA, *World Factbook, 1995*, "Kuwait"; World Bank, "A Population Perspective on Development: The Middle East and North Africa," August, 1994, p. 24.

75. "Special Report Kuwait," *Middle East Economic Digest*, February 24, 1995, pp. 9–22.

76. *Los Angeles Times*, January 28, 1992, p. C-1.

77. CIA, *World Factbook, 154*, "Kuwait."

Chapter 4

78. CIA, *World Factbook, 1995*, "Kuwait"; Based on the Internet version of the US State Department report on Human Rights for 1994, Kuwait country chapter, as accessed July 15, 1995 and March 9, 1996; and IEA, *Middle East Oil and Gas*, Paris, OECD/IEA, 1995, Annexes 1C and 2I.

79. Based on the Internet version of the US State Department report on Human Rights for 1994, Kuwait country chapter, as accessed July 15, 1995 and March 9, 1996; and IEA, *Middle East Oil and Gas*, Paris, OECD/IEA, 1995, Annexes 1C and 2I.

80. Based on the Internet version of the US State Department report on Human Rights for 1994, Kuwait country chapter, as accessed July 15, 1995 and March 9, 1996; and IEA, *Middle East Oil and Gas*, Paris, OECD/IEA, 1995, Annexes 1C and 2I.

81. Based on the Internet version of the US State Department report on Human Rights for 1994, Kuwait country chapter, as accessed July 15, 1995 and March 9, 1996; and IEA, *Middle East Oil and Gas*, Paris, OECD/IEA, 1995, Annexes 1C and 2I.

82. See Peter Carlson, "Castles in the Sand," *Washington Post Magazine,* January 14, 1996; Mary Tetrault, "Gulf Winds," *Current History,* 1996; F. Gregory Gause, *Oil Monarchies: Domestic and Security Challenges in the Arab Gulf States,* New York, Council on Foreign Relations, 1994.

83. Based on the Internet version of the US State Department report on Human Rights for 1994, Kuwait country chapter, as accessed July 15, 1995 and March 9, 1996; and IEA, Middle East Oil and Gas, Paris, OECD/IEA, 1995.

84. Based on the Internet version of the US State Department report on Human Rights for 1994, Kuwait country chapter, as accessed July 15, 1995 and March 9, 1996; and IEA, *Middle East Oil and Gas,* Paris, OECD/IEA, 1995, Annexes 1C and 2I.

85. *London Financial Times,* February 26, 1992, pp. III-1 to III-3. *The Sunday Times,* January 19, 1992, p. 1; *Time,* August 5, 1991, p. 32; Washington Times, May 27, 1992, p. A-7.

86. *London Financial Times,* February 26, 1992, pp. III-1 to III-3. *The Sunday Times,* January 19, 1992, p. 1; *Time,* August 5, 1991, p. 32; Washington Times, May 27, 1992, p. A-7.

87. Harry Brown, "Population Issues in the Middle East and North Africa," *RUSI Journal,* February, 1995, pp. 32–43.

88. *Middle East Economic Digest,* February 23, 1996, p. 11; Harry Brown, "Population Issues in the Middle East and North Africa," *RUSI Journal,* February, 1995, pp. 32–43; "CIA, *World Factbook, 1995,* "Kuwait."

89. CIA, *World Factbook, 1995,* "Kuwait."

90. *Middle East Economic Digest,* February 23, 1996, pp. 10–12.

91. Based on the Internet version of the US State Department report on Human Rights for 1994, Kuwait country chapter, as accessed July 15, 1995 and March 9, 1996; and IEA, *Middle East Oil and Gas,* Paris, OECD/IEA, 1995, Annexes 1C and 2I.

92. *Chicago Tribune,* November 3, 1991, p. I-14; *Washington Post,* November 7, 1991, p. 1, June 5, 1992, p. A-1, June 6, 1992, p. A-17, October 3, 1992, pp. A-13–14, October 6, 1992, p. A-18, October 7, p. A-27.; *Wall Street Journal,* October 24, 1992, p. A-2; Joseph P. Rive, "Kuwaiti Oil Well Fires Updated," Congressional Research Service, 91–313, June 26, 1991; *Washington Times,* May 28, 1992, p. A-7.

93. *Middle East Economic Digest,* February 24, 1995, pp. 9–22; Special Report Kuwait," February 24, 1995, pp. 9–22; June 16, 1995, p. 8; June 23, 1995, July 21, 1995, p. 11, August 11, 1995, pp. 10–11, August 25, 1995, p. 23, September 1, 1995, pp. 6–7; *Los Angeles Times,* June 27, 1995, p. C-3; *Jane's Defense Weekly,* July 29, 1995, pp. 17–18; *Washington Times,* August 2, 1995, p. A-16; *Boston Globe,* August 20, 1995, p. 2.

94. Based on the Internet version of the US State Department report on Human Rights for 1994, Kuwait country chapter, as accessed July 15, 1995 and March 9, 1996; and IEA, *Middle East Oil and Gas,* Paris, OECD/IEA, 1995, Annexes 1C and 2I.

95. Based on the Internet version of the US State Department report on Human Rights for 1994, Kuwait country chapter, as accessed July 15, 1995 and March 9, 1996; and IEA, *Middle East Oil and Gas,* Paris, OECD/IEA, 1995, Annexes 1C and 2I.

96. *Los Angeles Times,* June 27, 1995, p. C-3.

97. Amnesty International, *Report 1994*, New York, Amnesty International Publications, pp. 189–191.

Chapter 5

98. Reuters, August 5, 1995, 0353.

99. *Defense News*, April 18, 1995, p. 10; *Wall Street Journal*, June 27, 1995, p. A-10.

100. *Defense News*, March 2, 1992, p. 1; July, 1992, p. 29; *Armed Forces Journal*, July, 1992, p. 29.

Chapter 6

101. Arms Control and Disarmament Agency (ACDA), *World Military Expenditures and Arms Transfers, 1991–1992*, Washington, GPO, 1994, Table I, and ACDA computer print out, April, 14, 1996.

102. *Jane's Defense Weekly*, July 29, 1995, p. 18; *Washington Times*, August 2, 1995, p. A-16; IISS, *Military Balance, 1995–1996*, "Kuwait."

103. *Jane's Defense Weekly*, July 29, 1995, p. 18; *Washington Times*, August 2, 1995, p. A-16.

104. Arms Control and Disarmament Agency (ACDA), *World Military Expenditures and Arms Transfers, 1991–1992*, Washington, GPO, 1994, Table I, and ACDA computer print out, April, 14, 1996.

105. *Armed Forces Journal*, July, 1995, p. 25; *Jane's Defense Weekly*, July 29, 1995, p. 18; *Washington Times*, August 2, 1995, p. A-16.

106. *Defense News*, February 15, 1993, p. 1, April 18, 1994, p. 1, May 9, 1994, p. 12, December 13, 1993; *Jane's Defense Weekly*, October 29, 1994, p. 21; *Moneyclips*, July 4 and 8, 1993, Reuters European Business Report, February 24, 1993, July 8, 1993, August 21, 1993; Associated Press, January 29, 1993,

107. *Armed Forces International*, August, 1995, p. 22.

108. Arms Control and Disarmament Agency (ACDA), *World Military Expenditures and Arms Transfers, 1990*, Washington, GPO, 1993, Table III; Arms Control and Disarmament Agency (ACDA), *World Military Expenditures and Arms Transfers, 1993–1994*, Washington, GPO, 1995, Table III, and ACDA computer print out, April, 14, 1996.

109. Arms Control and Disarmament Agency (ACDA), *World Military Expenditures and Arms Transfers, 1991–1992*, Washington, GPO, 1994, Table II; Arms Control and Disarmament Agency (ACDA), *World Military Expenditures and Arms Transfers, 1993–1994*, Washington, GPO, 1995, Table II and ACDA computer print out, April, 14, 1996.

110. Arms Control and Disarmament Agency (ACDA), *World Military Expenditures and Arms Transfers, 1991–1992*, Washington, GPO, 1994, Table II; Arms Control and Disarmament Agency (ACDA), *World Military Expenditures and Arms Transfers, 1993–1994*, Washington, GPO, 1995, Table II and ACDA computer print out, April, 14, 1996.

111. Arms Control and Disarmament Agency (ACDA), *World Military Expenditures and Arms Transfers, 1994–1995*, Washington, GPO, 1996, Table III.

112. Richard F. Grimmett, *Conventional Arms Transfers to the Third World, 1986–1993*, CRS 94-612F, July 29, 1994, pp. 57–59; *Conventional Arms Transfers to the Third World, 1987–1994*, CRS 95-862F, August 4, 1994, pp. 56–69.

113. *Jane's Defense Weekly*, February 28, 1996, p. 3.

114. Richard F. Grimmett, *Conventional Arms Transfers to the Third World, 1986–1993*, CRS 94-612F, July 29, 1994, pp. 57–59; *Conventional Arms Transfers to the Third World, 1987–1994*, CRS 95-862F, August 4, 1994, pp. 56–69.

115. Richard F. Grimmett, *Conventional Arms Transfers to the Third World, 1986–1993*, CRS 94-612F, July 29, 1994, pp. 57–59; *Conventional Arms Transfers to the Third World, 1987–1994*, CRS 95-862F, August 4, 1994, pp. 56–69.

116. US Defense Security Assistance Agency (DSAA), "Foreign Military Sales, Foreign Military Construction Sales and Military Assistance Facts as of September 30, 1994," Department of Defense, Washington, 1995.

Chapter 7

117. CIA, *World Factbook, 1991*, pp. 173–174.

118. Kuwait is considering up-engining the tanks with new British or German engines. *Jane's Defense Weekly*, February 28, 1987, p. 323.

119. *Washington Times*, July 14, 1988, p. 2.

120. *Jane's Defense Weekly*, January 30, 1987, p. 151

121. *Jane's Defense Weekly*, February 28, 1987, p. 314 and March 7, 1987, p. 359.

122. I am indebted to Lt. Commander Jerry Ferguson, one of my students at Georgetown University, for much of the research, and many of the insights, on Gulf naval and air forces presented in this chapter.

123. The 76 mm and 40 mm guns can provide some air defense, but with little lethality. The TNC-45s have very complicated electronics, virtually all of which are maintained by foreign technicians. The voice network system used by the TNC-45 is so slow that it is virtually hopeless for air defense operations and generally creates confusion and increases delay and vulnerability if any attempt is made to use it.

124. Aircraft actually in storage included 12 Lightnings, 4 Hunters, and 9 BAC-167 Strikemasters.

125. The A-4s lack an air intercept radar, and can only engage in visual combat using guns or Sidewinder missiles. There are 12 Lightnings and 9 Hunters in storage.

126. *Defense News*, August 8, 1988, p. 7; *Jane's Defense Weekly*, August 13, 1988, p. 246; *Washington Times*, July 25, 1988, p. 1; *Newsweek*, August 25, 1988, p. 47.

127. Sources differ. The JCSS is shown. The IISS says 2 DC-9, 4 L-100-30.

Chapter 8

128. Major sources include Anthony H. Cordesman, *After the Storm: The Changing Military Balance in the Middle East*, Boulder, Westview, 1993; The IISS, *Military Balance, 1995–1996*, London, IISS, 1995; Tim Ripley, "Rebuilding the Kuwaiti Military," *International Defense Review*, 2/1993, pp. 157–159; Forecast International,

DMS Market Intelligence Report, Kuwait, June, 1994; James Bruce, "Kuwait: Castle in the Sand," *Jane's Defense Weekly*, October 29, 1994, p. 21, July 8, 1995, p. 15, July 29, 1995, pp. 17–36.

129. *Jane's Defense Weekly*, March 28, 1992, p. 531, July 29, 1995, pp. 17–36.

130. Estimates of Kuwait's restructured forces are based on material provided by the Kuwaiti Embassy, the Jaffee Center, the Congressional Research Service, and the IISS, *Military Balance, 1991–1992*, pp. 110–111 and *Military Balance, 1995–1996*, "Kuwait"; *New York Times*, January 14, 1992, p. 4; *London Financial Times*, February 26, 1992, p. III-1; *Defense News*, May 6, 1996, p. 29.

131. *New York Times*, May 24, 1991, p. 8; *London Financial Times*, June 21, 1992, p. 18.

132. *New York Times*, January 14, 1992, p. 4; *London Financial Times*, July 8, 1991, p. 3, February 26, 1992, p. III-1; *Jane's Defense Weekly*, December 14, 1991, p. 1174, July 29, 1995, pp. 17–36; *Armed Forces International*, August, 1993.

133. *Jane's Defense Weekly*, March 28, 1992, p. 531, July 29, 1995, pp. 17–36.

134. Major sources include Anthony H. Cordesman, *After the Storm: The Changing Military Balance in the Middle East*, Boulder, Westview, 1993; The *IISS Military Balance, 1995–1996*, London, IISS, 1995; Tim Ripley, "Rebuilding the Kuwaiti Military," *International Defense Review*, 2/1993, pp. 157–159; Forecast International, DMS Market Intelligence Report, Kuwait, June, 1994; James Bruce, "Kuwait: Castle in the Sand," *Jane's Defense Weekly*, October 29, 1994, p. 21, July 29, 1995, pp. 17–36.

135. *Washington Post*, January 11, 1995, p. A-12.

136. *Defense News*, February 10, 1992, p. 38.

137. The BMPs cost $700 million. IISS, *Military Balance, 1995–1996*, p. 138; *Jane's Defense Weekly*, July 29, 1995, p. 26.

138. *Defense News*, February 24, 1992, p. 1 & 82.

139. Iraq also retains a number of items that have potential military value, including 27 Hungarian buses, 100 Mercedes trucks, and 60 forklifts. *Washington Post*, January 11, 1995, p. A-12; *New York Times*, January 11, 1995, p. A-8.

140. *Armed Forces Journal*, July, 1995, p. 23.

Chapter 9

141. Major sources include Anthony H. Cordesman, *After the Storm: The Changing Military Balance in the Middle East*, Boulder, Westview, 1993; The *IISS Military Balance, 1995–1996*, London, IISS, 1995; Tim Ripley, "Rebuilding the Kuwaiti Military," *International Defense Review*, 2/1993, pp. 157–159; Forecast International, DMS Market Intelligence Report, Kuwait, June, 1994; James Bruce, "Kuwait: Castle in the Sand," *Jane's Defense Weekly*, October 29, 1994, p. 21, July 29, 1995, pp. 17–36.

142. IISS, *Military Balance, 1995–1996*, pp. 138–139; *Jane's Defense Weekly*, December 14, 1991, p. 1174; *London Financial Times*, November 18, 1991, p. 4; *Armed Forces Journal International*, April, 1994, p. 14.

143. *Defense News*, April 25, 1994; *Jane's Defense Weekly*, July 29, 1995, pp. 17–36.

144. *Defense News*, January 11, 1993, p. 3, February 27, p. 8; *Jane's Defense Weekly*, April 16, 1993, p. 8, August 20, 1994, p. 21, July 8, 1995, p. 15, July 29, 1995, pp. 17–36; *Kuwait in Brief*, November, 1995, p. 6.

145. *Jane's Defense Weekly*, March 28, 1992, p. 531, May 23, 1992, p. 878, May 30, 1992, p. 911, August 15, 1992, p. 5, September 5, 1992, p. 5, July 29, 1995, pp. 17–36; *London Financial Times*, July 8, 1991, p. 3; *Defense Week*, August 24, 1992, p. 1; *Defense News*, September 28, 1992, p. 18; *Armed Forces Journal*, November, 1992, p. 25.

146. The Warriors are being provided under a $794 million contract signed in August, 1993 with GKN Defense, a division of Telford, Inc. They will be specially modified to improved their performance in desert warfare, raising the cost to $918 million. *Defense News*, February 27, 1995, p. 8; July 8, 1995, p. 15, *Jane's Defense Weekly*, July 29, 1995, pp. 17–36.

147. *Jane's Defense Weekly*, July 29, 1995, pp. 17–36.

148. Kuwaiti law requires that contracts over one million dinars result in one-third of the value being reinvested in the Arab world, preferably in Kuwait. Executive News Service, July 25, 1995, 0941; August 30, 1995, 0809.

149. *Defense News*, January 11, 1993, p. 3, February 27, p. 8; *Jane's Defense Weekly*, April 16, 1993, p. 8, August 20, 1994, p. 21, July 8, 1995, p. 15, July 22, 1995, p. 17, July 29, 1995, pp. 17–36.

150. *Jane's Defense Weekly*, February 8, 1992, p. 187, February 22, 1992, p. 274, July 29, 1995, pp. 17–36; *Defense News*, November 18, 1991, p. 37; *London Financial Times*, February 16, 1992, p. 4.

151. *Jane's Defense Weekly*, March 28, 1992, pp. 530–531.

152. *Defense News*, May 6, 1996, p. 1.

153. *Jane's Defense Weekly*, July 22, 1995, p. 17.

154. The 12 round 300 mm Smerch was available at only $1.8 million per launcher and $140,000 per rocket and had twice the range of the MLRS. It did, however, have twice the reload time and required 25% more manpower, and only had one warhead with 72 conventional HE submunitions versus a choice of a warhead with 644 armor piercing submunitions or 28 anti-tank mines for the MLRS. Reuters European Business Report, January 6, 1993; *Defense News*, January 11, 1993, p. 3; *Jane's Defense Weekly*, April 16, 1993, p. 8, August 20, 1994, p. 21, July 29, 1995, pp. 17–36.

155. *Jane's Defense Weekly*, July 1, 1995, p. 27, July 29, 1995, pp. 17–36; *Armed Forces International*, August, 1995, p. 22.

156. *Defense News*, January 11, 1993, p. 3, February 27, p. 8; *Jane's Defense Weekly*, April 16, 1993, p. 8, August 20, 1994, p. 21, July 8, 1995, p. 15, July 29, 1995, pp. 17–36.

157. *Defense News*, November 18, 1991, p. 37, November 25, 1991, p. 22.

158. Associated Press, January 29, 1993; *New York Times*, October 11, 1994, October 30, 1994, p. 12; *Financial Times*, October 11, 1994, p. 5; *Army Times*, February 15, 1993, p. 24; *Jane's Defense Weekly*, March 28, 1992, p. 531.

Chapter 10

159. Major sources include Anthony H. Cordesman, *After the Storm: The Changing Military Balance in the Middle East*, Boulder, Westview, 1993; The *IISS Military Balance, 1995–1996*, London, IISS, 1995; Tim Ripley, "Rebuilding the Kuwaiti Military," *International Defense Review*, 2/1993, pp. 157–159; Forecast International,

DMS Market Intelligence Report, Kuwait, June, 1994; James Bruce, "Kuwait: Castle in the Sand," *Jane's Defense Weekly*, October 29, 1994, p. 21.

160. *Jane's Defense Weekly*, July 29, 1995, pp. 17–36.

161. *Jane's Defense Weekly*, February 22, 1992, p. 274; *Defense News*, November 18, 1991, p. 37, November 25, 1991, p. 22; *Jane's Fighting Ships, 1994*, London, Jane's, pp. 399–400.

162. *Jane's Fighting Ships, 1994*, London, Jane's, pp. 399–400.

163. IISS, *Military Balance, 1995–1996*, pp. 138–139; *International Defense Review*, 10/1991, p. 1152; *Armed Forces Journal*, April, 1994, p. 21; *Jane's Defense Weekly*, July 25, 1992; *Defense News*, August 24, 1994, pp. 3,36.

164. *Jane's Defense Weekly*, July 29, 1995, p. 30.

165. IISS, *Military Balance, 1995–1996*, pp. 138–139; *International Defense Review*, 10/1991, p. 1152, September 9, 1992, p. 802; *Armed Forces Journal*, April, 1994, p. 21; *Defense News*, April 18–24, 1994, p. 1, May 9, 1994, February 27, 1995, p. 6; *Jane's Defense Weekly*, January 15, 1994, p. 20, October 29, 1994, p. 21.

166. *Jane's Defense Weekly*, July 29, 1995, p. 30.

Chapter 11

167. Major sources include Anthony H. Cordesman, *After the Storm: The Changing Military Balance in the Middle East*, Boulder, Westview, 1993; The *IISS Military Balance, 1995–1996*, London, IISS, 1995; Tim Ripley, "Rebuilding the Kuwaiti Military," *International Defense Review*, 2/1993, pp. 157–159; Forecast International, DMS Market Intelligence Report, Kuwait, June, 1994; James Bruce, "Kuwait: Castle in the Sand," *Jane's Defense Weekly*, October 29, 1994, p. 21.

168. Full repairs were largely completed by the end of 1994. *Defense News*, November 18, 1991, p. 37.

169. Kuwait retains a stock of Matra 530 and 550 missiles, *Jane's Defense Weekly*, December 14, 1991, p. 1174; *Defense News*, November 18, 1991, p. 37; *Aviation Week*, November 14, 1994, p. 20.

170. *Aviation Week*, November 14, 1994, p. 20; *Defense News*, August 22, 1994, p. 8; *Jane's Exercise & Training Monitor, January–March 1996*, pp. 8–10, *Jane's Defense Weekly*, April 24, 1996, pp. 18–23.

171. The F/A-18s are the first delivered with the new F-404-GE-402 17,754 lb. thrust engines, giving it a 10–20% boost in power. IISS, *Military Balance, 1995–1996*, pp. 138–139; *St. Louis-Post Dispatch*, October 9, 1991, p. B-1; *Aviation Week*, February 3, 1992, p. 63, November 14, 1994, p. 20; *Jane's Defense Weekly*, October 26, 1991, p. 753, February 22, 1992, p. 274, March 28, 1992, p. 531, May 23, 1992, p. 879, April 24, 1996, pp. 18–22; *Washington Times*, March 29, 1993, p. A-2.

172. *Aviation Week*, November 14, 1994, p. 20; *Jane's Exercise & Training Monitor, January–March 1996*, pp. 8–10, *Jane's Defense Weekly*, April 24, 1996, pp. 18–23.

173. *Jane's Defense Weekly*, July 29, 1995, pp. 17–36, April 24, 1996, pp. 18–22.

174. The F/A-18s are the first delivered with the new F-404-GE-402 17,754 lb. thrust engines. IISS, *Military Balance, 1995–1996*, pp. 138–139; *St. Louis-Post Dispatch*, October 9, 1991, p. B-1; *Aviation Week*, February 3, 1992, p. 63, November 14,

1994, p. 20; *Jane's Defense Weekly*, October 26, 1991, p. 753, February 22, 1992, p. 274, March 28, 1992, p. 531, May 23, 1992, p. 879, July 29, 1995, pp. 17–36, April 24, 1996, pp. 18–22; *Washington Times*, March 29, 1993, p. A-2; *Jane's Exercise & Training Monitor, January–March 1996*, pp. 8–10.

175. *St. Louis-Post Dispatch*, October 9, 1991, p. B-1; *Aviation Week*, February 3, 1992, p. 63, November 14, 1994, p. 20; *Jane's Defense Weekly*, October 26, 1991, p. 753, April 24, 1996, pp. 18–22, February 22, 1992, p. 274, March 28, 1992, p. 531, May 23, 1992, p. 879, July 29, 1995, pp. 17–36; *Washington Times*, March 29, 1993, p. A-2; *Jane's Exercise & Training Monitor, January–March 1996*, pp. 8–10.

176. *Jane's Defense Weekly*, March 28, 1992, p. 530, July 29, pp. 17–36; Reuters, July 14, 1995, 1623.

177. *Defense News*, November 27–December 3, 1995, p. 4; *Jane's Defense Weekly*, July 29, pp. 4, and 17–36; Reuters, July 14, 1995, 1623; Executive News Service, July 14, 1995, 1623.

178. *Defense News*, November 27–December 3, 1995, p. 4.

179. *Aviation Week*, November 14, 1994, p. 20.

180. Jane's, *National and International Air Defense, 1994*, London, Jane's, p. 14.

181. *Flight International*, January 26, 1993, p. 5; *Wall Street Journal*, January 13, 1993, p. A-6; *International Defense Review*, 2/1993, p. 98; *Jane's Defense Weekly*, April 29, 1995, July 29, 1995, pp. 17–36.

182. *Kuwait in Brief*, March, 1996, p. 3.

183. *Flight International*, January 26, 1993, p. 5; *Wall Street Journal*, January 13, 1993, p. A-6; *International Defense Review*, 2/1993, p. 98; *Jane's Defense Weekly*, April 29, 1995, July 29, 1995, pp. 17–36.

184. *Flight International*, January 26, 1993, p. 5; *Wall Street Journal*, January 13, 1993, p. A-6; *International Defense Review*, 2/1993, p. 98; *Jane's Defense Weekly*, April 29, 1995, July 29, 1995, pp. 17–36.

185. IISS, *Military Balance, 1995–1996*, pp. 138–139; *Jane's Defense Weekly*, January 15, 1994, p. 20, October 29, 1994, p. 21, July 1, 1995, p. 27; *Defense News*, April 18–24, 1994, p. 1, May 9, 1994; Reuters, July 14, 1995, 1623.

Chapter 12

186. The following description of human rights is based on the Internet version of the US State Department report on Human Rights for 1994, Kuwait country chapter, and additional material from Middle East Watch and Amnesty International.

187. Based on the Internet version of the US State Department report on Human Rights for 1994 and 1995, Kuwait country chapter, as accessed July 15, 1995 and March 9, 1996.

188. Based on the Internet version of the US State Department report on Human Rights for 1994 and 1995, Kuwait country chapter, as accessed July 15, 1995 and March 9, 1996.

189. Based on the Internet version of the US State Department report on Human Rights for 1994 and 1995, Kuwait country chapter, as accessed July 15, 1995 and March 9, 1996

190. Based on the Internet version of the US State Department report on Human Rights for 1994 and 1995, Kuwait country chapter, as accessed July 15, 1995 and March 9, 1996.

191. Based on the Internet version of the US State Department report on Human Rights for 1994 and 1995, Kuwait country chapter, as accessed July 15, 1995 and March 9, 1996.

192. Based on the Internet version of the US State Department report on Human Rights for 1994 and 1995, Kuwait country chapter, as accessed July 15, 1995 and March 9, 1996.

193. Based on the Internet version of the US State Department report on Human Rights for 1994 and 1995, Kuwait country chapter, as accessed July 15, 1995 and March 9, 1996.

194. Based on the Internet version of the US State Department report on Human Rights for 1994 and 1995, Kuwait country chapter, as accessed July 15, 1995 and March 9, 1996.

195. Based on the Internet version of the US State Department report on Human Rights for 1994 and 1995, Kuwait country chapter, as accessed July 15, 1995 and March 9, 1996.

196. Based on the Internet version of the US State Department report on Human Rights for 1994 and 1995, Kuwait country chapter, as accessed July 15, 1995 and March 9, 1996.

197. Based on the Internet version of the US State Department report on Human Rights for 1994 and 1995, Kuwait country chapter, as accessed July 15, 1995 and March 9, 1996.

198. Based on the Internet version of the US State Department report on Human Rights for 1994 and 1995, Kuwait country chapter, as accessed July 15, 1995 and March 9, 1996.

199. Based on the Internet version of the US State Department report on Human Rights for 1994 and 1995, Kuwait country chapter, as accessed July 15, 1995 and March 9, 1996.

200. Based on the Internet version of the US State Department report on Human Rights for 1994 and 1995, Kuwait country chapter, as accessed July 15, 1995 and March 9, 1996.

Chapter 13

201. *New York Times*, October 28, 1994, p. A-3.

202. Deutsche Press-Agentur, November 21, 1994; November 30, 1994; *Jane's Defense Weekly*, July 9, 1992; *Jane's Exercise & Training Monitor*, January–March 1996, pp. 8–9.

203. *Jane's Defense Weekly*, February 22, 1992, p. 274, March 7, 1992, p. 375, August 1, 1992, p. A-10, August 4, 1992, p. A-14, August 8, 1992, p. 6, August 15, 1992, p. A-15; *Defense News*, September 9, 1991, p. 1, November 18, 1991, p. 3, February 17, 1992, p. 3, June 15, 1992, p. 26; *Stars and Stripes*, March 3, 1992, p. 8; *London Financial Times*, July 8, 1991, p. 3; *Washington Post*, August 28, 1991, p. A-7, September 6, 1991, p. A-24, August 15, 1992, p. A-15; *Washington Times*,

December 6, 1991, p. A-2, August 5, 1992, p. A-1; *Aviation Week*, September 9, 1991, p. 21.

204. Chalupa-BG R's SORG FS Brief; *New York Times*, October 14, 1994, p. A-1; *Washington Post*, October 14, 1994, p. A-33; Department of Defense background briefing, October 20, 1994 (Federal News Service); Department of Defense handouts of October 11, 1994 and October 12, 1994; *Jane's Defense Weekly*, October 22, 1994, p. 4, December 17, 1994, p. 7; US Army briefing sheet (undated) October, 1994; Congressional Research Service, *Iraq Crisis, October, 1994, A Chronology*, 94-808F, October 24, 1994; *Jane's Defense Weekly*, July 29, 1995, pp. 22–24.

205. *Washington Times*, August 29, 1995; *Jane's Defense Weekly*, August 26, 1995, p. 3.

206. Executive News Service, August 29, 1995, 0329, September 19, 1995, 1014, September 27, 1995, 0324; *Washington Post*, August 19, 1995, p. A-17;

207. *New York Times*, January 30, 1996, p. A-6.

208. Deutsche Press-Agentur, November 21, 1994; November 30, 1994; *Jane's Defense Weekly*, July 9, 1992.

209. *New York Times*, October 14, 1994, p. A-1; *Washington Post*, October 14, 1994, p. A-33; Department of Defense background briefing, October 20, 1994 (Federal News Service); Congressional Research Service, *Iraq Crisis, October, 1994, A Chronology*, 94-808F, October 24, 1994; *Jane's Defense Weekly*, July 29, 1995, pp. 22–24; *Jane's Exercise & Training Monitor*, January–March 1996, pp. 8–9.

210. *New York Times*, October 14, 1994, p. A-1; *Washington Post*, October 14, 12994, p. A-33; Congressional Research Service, *Iraq Crisis, October, 1994, A Chronology*, 94-808F, October 24, 1994; *Jane's Defense Weekly*, July 29, 1995, pp. 22–24; *Jane's Exercise & Training Monitor*, January–March, 1996, pp. 8–9.

Sources and Methods

This volume is part of a series of volumes on each of the Gulf states which has been developed by the Center for Strategic and International Studies as part of a dynamic net assessment of the Middle East. This project has had the sponsorship of each of the Southern Gulf states as well as US sponsors of the CSIS, and each text has been widely distributed for comment to experts and officials in each Southern Gulf country, to US experts and officials, and to several international agencies and institutions, and various private experts.

Sources

The author has drawn heavily on the inputs of outside reviewers throughout the text. It was agreed with each reviewer, however, that no individual or agency should be attributed at any point in the text except by specific request, and that all data used be attributed to sources that are openly available to the public. The reader should be aware of this in reviewing the footnotes. Only open sources are normally referred to in the text, although the data contained in the analysis has often been extensively modified to reflect expert comment.

There are other aspects of the sources used of which the reader should be aware. It was possible to visit each Southern Gulf states at various times during the preparation of this book and to talk to local officials and experts. Some provided detailed comments on the text. Interviews also took place with experts in the United States, United Kingdom, France, Switzerland and Germany. Portions of the manuscript were circulated for informal review by European officials and diplomats in some cases. Once again, no details regarding such visits or comments are referenced in the text.

Data from open sources are deliberately drawn from a wide range of sources. Virtually all of these sources are at least in partial conflict. There is no consensus over demographic data, budget data, military expenditures and arms transfers, force numbers, unit designations, or weapons types.

While the use of computer data bases allowed some cross-correlation and checking of such source, the reporting on factors like force strengths, unit types and identities, tactics often could not be reconciled and citing multiple sources for each case was not possible because it involved many detailed judgments by the author in reconciling different reports and data.

The Internet and several on-line services were also used extensively. Since such the data bases are dynamic, and change or are deleted over time, there is no clear way to footnote much of this material. Recent press sources are generally cited, but are often only part of the material consulted.

Methods

A broad effort has been made to standardize the analysis of each country, but it became clear early in the project that adopting a standard format did not suit the differences that emerged between countries. The emphasis throughout this phase of the CSIS net assessment has been on analyzing the detailed trends within individual states and this aspects of the analysis has been given priority over country-to-country consistency.

In many cases, the author adjusted the figures and data use in the analysis on a "best guess" basis, drawing on some thirty years of experience in the field. In some other cases, the original data provided by a given source were used without adjustment to ensure comparability, even though this leads to some conflicts in dates, place names, force strengths, etc. within the material presented—particularly between summary tables surveying a number of countries and the best estimates for a specific country in the text. In such cases, it seemed best to provide contradictory estimates to give the reader some idea of the range of uncertainty involved.

Extensive use is made of graphics to allow the reader to easily interpret complex statistical tables and see long-term trends. The graphic program used was deliberately standardized, and kept relatively simple, to allow the material portrayed to be as comparable as possible. Such graphics have the drawback, however, that they often disguise differences in scale and exaggerate or minimize key trends. The reader should carefully examine the scale used in the left-hand axis of each graphs.

Most of the value judgments regarding military effectiveness are made on the basis of American military experience and standards. Although the author has lived in the Middle East, and worked as a US advisor to several Middle Eastern governments, he believes that any attempt to create some Middle Eastern standard of reference is likely to be far more arbitrary than basing such judgments on his own military background.

Mapping and location names presented a major problem. The author used US Army and US Air Force detailed maps, commercial maps, and in some cases commercial satellite photos. In many cases, however, the place names and terrain descriptions used in the combat reporting by both sides, and by independent observers, presented major contradictions that could not be resolved from available maps. No standardization emerged as to the spelling of place names. Sharp differences emerged in the geographic data published by various governments, and in the conflicting methods of transliterating Arabic and Farsi place names into English.

The same problem applied in reconciling the names of organizations and individuals—particularly those being transliterated from Arabic and Farsi. It again became painfully obvious that no progress is being made in reconciling the conflicting methods of transliterating such names into English. A limited effort has been made to standardize the spellings used in this text, but many different spellings are tied to the relational data bases used in preparing the analysis and the preservation of the original spelling is necessary to identify the source and tie it to the transcript of related interviews.

About the Book and Author

With the thoroughness that this recently spotlighted nation requires, this volume examines Kuwait's internal and external security situation after the turbulent days of the Gulf War and investigates continued Western involvement in its safekeeping. It also examines Kuwait's changing role as an energy exporter.

Anthony H. Cordesman has served in senior positions in the office for the secretary of defense, NATO, and the U.S. Senate. He is currently a senior fellow and Co-Director of the Middle East Program at the Center for Strategic and International Studies, an adjunct professor of national security studies at Georgetown University, and a special consultant on military affairs for ABC News. He lives in Washington, D.C.